# History Source Books

## The Elizabethan Age Book 3

# The Poor and the Wicked

Peter & Mary Speed

Oxford University Press 1987

**Oxford University Press, Walton Street, Oxford OX2 6DP**

Oxford   New York   Toronto
Delhi   Bombay   Calcutta   Madras   Karachi
Petaling Jaya   Singapore   Hong Kong   Tokyo
Nairobi   Dar es Salaam   Cape Town
Melbourne   Auckland

and associated companies in
Beirut   Berlin   Ibadan   Nicosia

*Oxford* is a trade mark of Oxford University Press

© Peter & Mary Speed 1987

ISBN 0 19 917115 7

Typeset by Best-set Typesetter Limited, Hong Kong
Printed in Hong Kong

## Acknowledgements

The publishers would like to thank the following for permission
to reproduce the photographs:

BBC Hulton Picture Library, pp 23, 63, 76; Bodleian Library,
pp 3 & 49 (Mal 575 (2) TP), 39 (Roxburghe Ballads), 44 (4°R 21
Art Seld (6) TP), 49 (Mal 575 (2) TP), 58 (Mal 669 D.1.v), 62
right (4°E17 (13) Art TP); Bridewell Royal Hospital/King Edward
School, Witley, p 19; Bridgeman Art Library, pp 50, 78 (Victoria
& Albert Museum); British Library, pp 11 centre (Add MS
28330), 22, 33, right, 42 (MS 55046); Trustees of the British
Museum, pp 33 left, 35, 36, 62 top left; Board of Directors of the
Budapest Museum of Fine Arts, p 38; The Syndics of Cambridge
University Library, p 26 (J. Wodderspoon 'Memorials of the
Ancient Town of Ipswich' 1850); C.W. Cunnington & P
Cunnington 'Handbook of English Costume in the Sixteenth
Century' Faber & Faber 1970, pp 10 left and 11 left; Fotomas
Index, p 10 right; Graphische Sammlung Albertina, Vienna, p 5;
Guildhall Library, City of London, pp 20, 66 left; Peter Haining
'The Witchcraft Papers' Robert Hale, pp 73, 77; Ipswich
Museums and Galleries, p 26 centre; Trevor James, p 30; Simon
King, Oundle School, p 17; Kunsthistorisches Museum, Vienna,
pp 7, 9, 75; The Master and Fellows, Magdalene College,
Cambridge, p 64; Mansell Collection, pp 13, 57, 65; Musées
Royaux des Beaux-Arts de Belgique, Brussels, p 54; The
Museum of London, pp 8, 46, 48, 66 right, 71; National Gallery,
Prague, p 11 right; National Trust Photographic Library/Jon
Gibson, p 63 top; L F Salzman 'England in Tudor Times'
Batsford, p 69; Scala, p 27; Peter Speed, pp 14, 47, 62 bottom, 63
bottom left; Suffolk Record Office, Ipswich, pp 25, 28

Illustrations by Nick Hawken and Christine Molan

# Contents

Conny-catching.

# 1 The Poor

## A Introduction

There were a great many poor people in Elizabethan England. We will ask a man called Henry Arth to tell us why.

*'Whose fault is it, that you have so many poor?'*

'Partly, it is the fault of the poor themselves. Partly it is the fault of some of the rich. Partly it is the fault of us all.'

*'How are the poor to blame?'*

'They make God angry in a number of ways. In the first place, they are sometimes idle. They will not work, even if they have the chance. Secondly, when they do have a little money, they will not save any. Instead, they waste it, over-eating and getting drunk. Thirdly, I am sorry to say, they do not lead good lives. They grumble and curse and swear a great deal. Above all, they do not go to church often enough.'

*'How are rich people to blame?'*

'They are not all to blame. But some of them make other folk poor by their thoughtless deeds.'

*'Who does that?'*

'First of all, there are those who waste their money. They buy expensive clothes. They eat and drink too much. They lose large sums by gambling. If they did none of these things, they could give the money they saved to the poor. Secondly, some employers are selfish. Farmers sack workers they no longer need. Gentlemen sack servants, to save paying their wages. Craftsmen sack their apprentices, even though they have promised to keep them for seven years. Thirdly, corn dealers are greedy. They buy all the corn they can and lock it away. Then, they refuse to sell it until the price is high enough to please them. Meanwhile, poor people are hungry.'

*'You also said that everyone is to blame. How can that be?'*

'We are a wicked race, and God is punishing us. He has made Spain our enemy. She is the most powerful country in the world. He has sent us the Black Death, which kills many, and terrifies the rest. Moreover He has given us the poor, to be a burden on us.'

1  According to Henry Arth, whose fault is it that there are so many poor people in England? (He names three groups.)
2  What do the poor sometimes do when they have the chance to work?
3  What do they do when they have some money?
4  In what ways do they lead bad lives?
5  How do some rich people waste money?
6  What should they do with it, instead?
7  What do some employers do to their workers?
8  Why do corn dealers keep their corn locked away?
9  How do poor people suffer meanwhile?
10  Why is God punishing the English?
11  In what three ways is He doing so?

Henry Arth was a real man. You have been looking at some of the ideas he wrote in his book, *Provision for the Poore, 1597*. Some of these ideas seem strange to us. Look at the last paragraph. Today, we might blame the government when things go wrong. Not many of us would blame God! But you must remember that Henry Arth lived four hundred years ago. In those days, people did not think in quite the same way that we do.

Henry Arth does not mention one other important reason why people were poor. This was bad harvests, which happened from time to time. For example, the harvest of 1586 was very bad. Then, between 1594 and 1598, the harvest failed for five years in a row. This brought hunger everywhere in England and, in some parts, famine.

**Figure 1**
The Fat Kitchen

**Figure 2**
The Thin Kitchen
Brueghel's pictures show the difference between those who had enough to eat and those who did not.

# B   Food of the Poor

Most of the time, the poor did not eat well. Mainly, they lived on bread. A clergyman called William Harrison wrote:

*Document One*
All over England, the rich provide themselves with wheat bread, while their poor neighbours in some counties have to be content with rye or barley bread. Yea, and in time of shortage, many have bread made of beans, peas or oats, and some acorns among. The price of corn is so high that the poor man is driven to eat horse-corn, I mean beans, peas, oats, and lentils. And therefore it is a true proverb that, 'Hunger setteth his first foot in the horse manger.'
*The Description of Britaine*, 1578

1   What bread do rich people all over England eat?
2   What bread do poor people eat, in some parts of England?
3   What do poor people use to make bread when food is short?
4   What does Harrison mean by 'horsecorn'? Would you object to eating it?

Harrison thinks it dreadful that poor people must eat rye or barley bread. Today, we have to pay high prices for such bread in health food shops! This shows how ideas on food can change.

Since the poor lived mainly on bread, its price was very important to them. In fact, the price of a loaf did not change. It was always one penny. What did change was the weight of the loaf. This is what it was in certain years:

1558 – 56 ounces
1560 – 36 ounces
1597 –   8 ounces

Today, a large loaf is 28 ounces.

1   How many of our loaves could be bought for one penny in 1558?
2   What fraction of one of our loaves, roughly, could be bought for one penny in 1597? ($\frac{8}{28} = ?$)

3   A poor man might earn no more than £5 a year. There were 240 old pennies in £1, so £5 was 1200 old pennies. Assume the man spends all his wages on bread:
   **a**   How many of our loaves would he have bought in the whole of 1558? How many, roughly, would that have been every day. (To make your arithmetic easier, say there are 360 days in a year.)
   **b**   How many loaves could the man have bought in 1597? ($\frac{1200 \times 8}{28} = ?$)

How many, roughly, would that have been every day?

You can see that in 1558, £5 bought more bread than a normal family could eat. That meant they had money for other things.

In 1597, even if they spent every penny on bread, they still went hungry.

The main reason for the big changes in the price of bread was the harvest. A good harvest meant cheap bread, and a poor harvest meant dear bread. There was a run of bad harvests from 1594 to 1598. This was a dreadful time for the poor. You can read about it in Shakespeare's *A Midsummer Night's Dream* Act 2, Scene 2, lines 87–114.

It was not only food which was simple. This is all that one poor man had in the way of cooking equipment, crockery and cutlery. He was Thomas Herries, who died at Norwich in 1599. The list shows the values of the items in old money:

*Document Two*

| | |
|---|---|
| A frying pan, a pair of tongs and a roasting iron. | 1s-6d |
| One little kettle and 3 pewter spoons | 2s-6d |
| 3 little bowls | 1s-0d |
| One kettle, one pot spoon | 1s-0d |
| 2 wooden platters and 5 dishes and 2 earthen pots | 8d |
| 5 stoneware pots | 4d |

*Inventory of Thomas Herries*

**Figure 1** Peasant Feast

Once in a while, poor people could afford a feast. William Harrison tells us what they ate:

*Notes*: A kettle was used to cook food, not just to boil water.
'platter' – plate
'inventory' – list of a person's goods, made when he died

1 The total value of the things on the list, in old money, is 7s-0d. This might be worth about £40 today. Ask a parent to tell you how much all the cooking equipment, crockery and cutlery in your home are worth. Certainly the oven alone will be worth far more than £40.

2 What is the only cutlery mentioned here? (Thomas Herries would also have eaten with the same knife that he carried everywhere.)

3 What did Thomas Herries and his family use for plates?

4 What did they drink from?

*Document Three*
Their food consists mainly in beef and such meat as the butcher sells – that is to say, mutton, veal, lamb, pork, etc, besides bacon, fruit, pies of fruit, fowls of different sorts, cheese, butter, eggs, etc.

In feasting, it is amazing what food is eaten, each one bringing a dish with him. It is commonly seen at these banquets that the host finds nothing save bread, drink, sauce and fire.

Both the artificer and the husbandman are very friendly at their tables. When they meet, they are so merry that it is good to be among them. The poor are only to be blamed in that their talk is now and then such as savoureth of scurrility and ribaldry, a thing natural to carters and clowns.

At their meetings, if they have a piece of venison and a cup of wine or very strong beer, they think they have fared as well as the Lord Mayor of London.
*The Description of Britaine*, 1578

**Figure 1** Earthenware kettle for cooking food. Why does it have legs, do you think?

*Notes*: 'finds' – provides
'artificer' – workman
'husbandman' – peasant
'their talk savoureth of scurrility and ribaldry' – they tell rude stories and jokes

**1** What are some of the meats that poor people have?

**2** What other food do they have?

**3** Sugar was expensive. Harrison mentions only one dish that was likely to contain it. Which is that? (Probably, it was sweetened with honey, anyway.)

**4** What does each guest bring to the banquet?

**5** What are the only things which the host has to provide?

**6** What does Harrison like about the way poor people behave at table?

**7** What does he dislike? (Remember that Harrison was a clergyman!)

**8** What do poor people enjoy particularly?

Harrison also wrote:

*Document Four*
The poorer husbandmen and country folk are given to very much babbling. Among them he is thought to be the merriest who talks the most ribaldry, or the wisest man, he that speaks fastest. Now and then there is overeating and drunkenness among them. It may be that some of them living at home with hard and pinching diet soonest give way to temptation when they come into such banquets
*The Description of Britaine*, 1578

*Note*: 'hard and pinching diet' – little to eat

**1** What do poor people think of anyone who tells lots of rude stories? (ribaldry)

**2** What do they think of anyone who talks fast?

**3** Harrison says that poor people sometimes eat and drink too much at banquets. What excuse does he make for them?

## C   Homes of the Poor

In the sixteenth century, houses that poor people built for themselves were badly made, and none is standing today. Such a house was certainly very simple, with no more than two rooms. There might be a loft over one of them, reached by a ladder.

Fortunately we know more about the household goods of poor people. This is because, when anyone died, there had to be an 'inventory', or list of all his possessions. Some of these inventories have survived.

You have already seen part of the inventory of Thomas Herries, the poor man who died at Norwich in 1599. Here is the rest:

*Document One*

| | |
|---|---|
| One boarded bedstead | 3s-4d |
| One mattress | 1s-6d |
| One flock bed | 2s-6d |
| One bolster | 2s-0d |
| One feather pillow and an old cushion | 1s-6d |
| 2 leather pillows filled with feathers | 3s-4d |
| One pair of sheets | 2s-0d |
| One bed blanket | 1s-8d |
| An old chest | 2s-0d |
| One empty barrel | 3d |
| 2 salt boxes | 1s-0d |

**Figure 2**  Peasant Home  The man sitting at the table is not one of the family. In what ways is this house uncomfortable?

| | |
|---|---|
| A hamper and certain old washing | 6d |
| 2 stools | 6d |
| A little table and 4 stools | 3s-0d |
| 3 chisels and 2 hammers | 8d |
| 3 old cushions | 6d |
| 2 pairs of cuffs, and one dozen handkerchiefs and an old pillowcase | 2s-6d |
| 2 old shirts | 1s-8d |
| One old form and 2 old caps | 1s-0d |

*Inventory of Thomas Herries*

*Notes*: 'flock bed' – soft mattress stuffed with waste wool. It was put over the hard straw mattress to make it more comfortable. Rich people had feather beds.

'salt boxes' – people used a lot of salt to preserve their food.

The list does not give all of Thomas Herries's clothes. Probably, the rest was not worth anything.

1  The total value of these goods is £1-11s-5d, which was worth, perhaps, £200 in our money. Ask a parent how much all your family's furniture and clothing are worth.

2  The total value of the bed and bedding is 18s-10d, which is worth, perhaps, £120 in our money. How does this compare with the value of all the other goods that Thomas Herries had? (Including the cooking equipment, crockery and cutlery which you saw in the last section, the total value was about £240 in our money.)
How does the value of your beds and bedding compare with the value of the rest of your household goods, do you think?

3  What did Thomas Herries and his family sit on?

4  How did they make them more comfortable?

9

## D Clothes of the Poor

A writer called Fynes Moryson describes the materials in the clothes of working people:

*Document One*
Husbandmen wear garments of coarse woollen cloth, made at home, and their wives, gowns of the same, kirtles of some light stuff, with linen aprons. Their linen is coarse and made at home.
*The Itinerary*, 1605

*Note*: 'kirtle' – skirt

1 What are the materials working folk wear?
2 Where is the cloth made?

Figure 1 shows some pictures of working men. Each of them is wearing a 'cote'. This is a loose, belted garment reaching below the hips. The groom's is fastened with laces, called 'points', but the ploughman has a single button. The gardener has found an extra use for his belt. What is that? Probably, all these men are wearing linen shirts beneath their cotes.

On his legs, the groom is wearing hose, rather like tights. The gardener has loose breeches, open at the bottom.

**Figure 1** Gardener, Groom and Ploughman

Both the gardener and the groom are wearing shoes. For his much heavier work the ploughman has big boots, with thick soles. They are done up with a strap. He has oversocks to keep his legs warm. None of the men has heels on his shoes. Heels were uncommon before 1600.

Today, it is often possible to tell someone's occupation from his dress. For example, there is no mistaking a policeman, a fireman or a bus driver. Such differences were only just beginning to show in Elizabethan times, and mainly in aprons. Aprons themselves were quite new, and, gradually, different trades started to have their own styles. Millers and cooks wore white aprons; barbers had checkered aprons; men like builders and blacksmiths, who did heavy work, had leather aprons. This is an extract from Shakespeare's *Julius Caesar*:

What trade art thou?
Why, Sir, a carpenter.

**Figure 2**  Farm Servant and Peasant's Wife

**Figure 3**  Peasant Girls going Haymaking. Compare the dress of these girls with that of the women in Figure 2. Note the wide brimmed hats. It was unfashionable to have a sun tan.

Where is thy leather apron and thy rule? Figure 2 shows pictures of two working women. The girl on the left is, perhaps, a farm servant. She is working indoors. On her head she just has a kerchief to keep her hair clean and tidy. She has a plain bodice, opening at the front, and tight sleeves. She has something draped rather untidily over her shoulders, and we cannot tell if it is a garment or not. It might be a neckerchief, or it might be a cloth of some kind connected with her work. She has a long, straight skirt, or kirtle. What is she wearing to protect it? From what materials are her clothes made, do you think?

A fashionable woman would have puffed out her shoulders and sleeves; she would have worn a system of hoops called a far-thingale to make her skirt stand out from her body; she would have squeezed her waist to make it look as slim as possible; she would have worn expensive garments covered in ornaments and jewels. The working girl does none of these things. Why not?

The woman on the right is, perhaps, a peasant's wife. She is outdoors and she is going to market, so she is doing her best to look smart and keep warm. She has a tall hat and, underneath it, a white coif. This fits closely to her head. Probably, it is the same one that she wears in bed. To keep her face warm she has a muffler, or 'chin-clout'. She has a ruff round her neck, and matching ruffs round her wrists. A fashionable lady would have the same, except that her neck ruff would be much bigger.

On her shoulders, the peasant woman has a short cape, called a 'tippet'. She is also wearing a full length gown. Below her waist it opens, probably in a long, narrow ∧ to show her kirtle. You can just see the opening at the bottom. The woman must be proud of her gown, but she is behaving very differently from a lady of fashion. A rich woman would want to show off her best garment. The peasant woman thinks more of protecting it, so she hides her gown under a long, white apron.

11

# 2  Care of the Poor

## A  Introduction

Some rich Elizabethans did a great deal to help the poor. The London merchants were particularly generous. We will talk to one of them. His name is John Finch.

*'Is much money given to charity?'*

'A very great deal.'

*'Is this something new?'*

'No, but there have been changes. Charities were very different, even fifty years ago.'

*'What has happened?'*

'I think the most important thing is that people no longer give to the Church. Instead, they give to the poor.'

*'Why is that?'*

'Before the reign of Henry VIII we were a Catholic country. Catholics believe in praying for the souls of the dead. It was thought a good idea to give plenty of money to the Church. Then, priests would pray for your soul. But we are a Protestant country now. We do not believe that our prayers can do much for the dead. As a result, we help the needy in this world. We leave the souls who are in the next world to the care of God.'

*'Have there been any other changes?'*

'Yes. We are more careful of the way we give help. In the old days, people liked to make a show with generous gifts. For example, when a man called William Paston died, he left £100 to buy food for any poor people who came to his funeral. Of course, a huge crowd of a thousand people appeared. A day later, though, they were hungry again, and the money was all spent.'

*'What should William Paston have done?'*

'He should have left land worth £100 for the use of the poor. A farmer will pay £5 rent a year for such a piece of land.'

*'£5 is not much.'*

'No, but it will buy enough food for two old people for a year. Also, there will be £5 every year for as long as the land is there. Is it better to pay for a thousand people to make pigs of themselves for one day, or to find enough food for two old folk for ever?'

*'What exactly is done with the money you give?'*

'Much of it is used to build almshouses and hospitals.'

*'What are almshouses?'*

'They are houses which are given, rent free, to people who are too old to work, but still able to look after themselves. Of course, we only give almshouses to those who deserve them. They must have led good lives, and gone regularly to church.'

*'It is a good idea to give such people homes. But how do they find food?'*

'Every one of them has a small pension. It may not be much, but it will buy them enough food to keep them alive.'

*'Have you given anything for almshouses yourself?'*

'I have indeed. In my will I have left money for the building of ten almshouses. They will be a fine memorial to me. They will have a large endowment, too.'

*'What is it?'*

'It is two farms which I have in Hertfordshire. They are let to farmers who pay good, fair rents for them. The rents will pay for the repair of the almshouses. They will also pay the pensions of the almsmen. The land will last for ever. The rents will come in for ever. My almshouses will last for ever. There will be ten almsmen to bless my name until the end of the world.'

**Figure 1** Doctor and Patient   The doctor is examining a specimen of the patient's urine.

*'You also mentioned hospitals. Who are they for?'*

'They are for people who are unable or unwilling to look after themselves. We divide them into three groups. First, there are the impotent poor. They are the ones who are helpless. They include the sick, of course, who go to hospital to be cured. But many are impotent for other reasons than sickness. They may be very old, or blind, or lame. The impotent poor have two hospitals, St. Bartholomew's and St. Thomas's. The second group is orphan children, who have no home but the streets. These we take into Christ's Hospital. The third group is strong, lusty rogues and beggars. They could quite well work, but will not do so. These we take into Bridewell Hospital. There, they are made to work. If they do not, they are whipped.'

1   Why did people give a lot of money to the Church before the reign of Henry VIII? (He was king from 1509 to 1547.)

2   Who has the money now?

3   How much money did William Paston leave the poor? How many did it feed? For how long?

4   According to John Finch, what should William Paston have done? How many poor people would have been fed, as a result? For how long?

5   Which people have almshouses?

6   How are people in almshouses able to buy food?

7   John Finch has given his almshouses an endowment of two farms. How will the rent from these farms be spent?

8   How long does John Finch think his almshouses will last?

9   John Finch divides the poor into three groups. His first group is the 'impotent poor.' Who are they?

10   Which are the hospitals for the impotent poor?

11   Which is the hospital for orphan children?

12   Where are lazy people sent? What happens to them there?

# B Charities

Study the following table. The figures are for the county of Norfolk. They show how the money given to charity was shared at different times. The figures are not the actual amounts, but percentages, which are easier to compare.

|  | Poor | Education | Religion | Other |
|---|---|---|---|---|
| Early Sixteenth Century | 12% | 11% | 60% | 17% |
| Late Sixteenth Century | 44% | 30% | 8% | 18% |

1 You can see from the table that two kinds of charity were taking much bigger shares by the end of the century. Which were they?
2 You can see that one kind of charity had a much smaller share by the end of the century. Which one is that?
3 Imagine you have a large sum of money to give to a poor country in Africa. You can use it to:
   a help the poor
   b build a school
   c build a church.

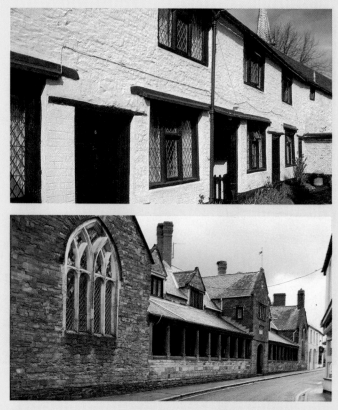

**Figure 1** Almshouses at Barnstaple   The picture above shows a group of almshouses. They are built round a courtyard, though here you can only see the outside. There are two chapels, one at either end, with a covered walk joining them. The entrance to the courtyard is in the middle. The picture below shows the inside of the courtyard. In the middle of the courtyard is a pump. The picture at the top shows a more modest group of almshouses, in another part of the town.

Which will you choose to do? Why?
Which will be your second choice?
Now look back at the table. Do you agree more with the people of the early part of the sixteenth century, or those of the later part?

4   If you know about pie diagrams, draw two to show the information given in the table.

John Stow describes one of the London charities of the later sixteenth century. It was given by Sir John Milborn, a wealthy draper:

*Document One*
He appointed every Sunday for ever, thirteen penny loaves of white bread to be given in the parish church of St. Edmund in Lombard Street, to thirteen poor people of that parish; and the like thirteen loaves to be given in the parish church of St. Michael upon Cornhill; and in either parish every year one load of coal, of thirty sacks in the load; and this gift to be continued for ever; for the endowment whereof, he gave twenty-three messuages and eighteen garden plots, in the parish of St. Olave.
*A Survey of London*

*Note*:   'messuage' – house and garden

1   Under this charity, what is to be given to the poor every week?
2   What are they to have every year?
3   You can see that Sir John Milborn wants his charity to go on 'for ever'. So that there will always be money for it, he gives it an endowment. What is this endowment?

John Stow tells us what some of the other rich merchants of London gave to charity:

*Document Two*
**Sir William Laxton**, Grocer, Mayor 1545, founded a fair free school at Oundle with six alms houses for the poor.
**Sir Thomas White**, merchant tailor, Mayor 1556, founded St. John's College, Oxford, and gave great sums of money to several towns in England for the relief of the poor.
**William Harpur**, merchant tailor, Mayor 1562, founded a free school in the town of Bedford where he was born.
**William Lamb**, Gentleman and Clothworker, in the year 1577 builded a water conduit at Oldborne Cross to his charges of £1500.
**Richard May**, Merchant Taylor, gave £300 towards the new building of Blackwell Hall in London, a market place for woollen cloth.
**Sir Thomas Roe**, Merchant Taylor, Mayor 1568, gave to the Merchant Taylors lands and houses, out of them to be given to ten poor men, Clothworkers, Carpenters, Tilers, Plasterers and Armourers, £40 yearly, namely £4 each. Also £100 to be lent to eight poor men. Besides, he enclosed with a wall of brick one acre of ground belonging to the Hospital of Bethlem, to be a burial for the dead.
**Anne Gibson**, widow unto Nicholas Gibson, grocer, founded a free school at Ratcliff near unto London, appointing to the same for the instruction of 60 poor men's children, a Schoolmaster and Usher. She also built almshouses for 14 poor aged persons, each of them to receive quarterly 6s-8d for ever.
*A Survey of London*

*Notes*:   The schools at Oundle and Bedford are still there today. Both are important and famous.
'conduit' – water supply
'Bethlem' – a hospital for the insane

1   Which of these merchants gave money to help the poor?
2   Which of them gave money for education?
3   Some of the merchants gave money for town improvements. Which were they, and what improvements did they pay for?

Due to bad harvests, there were serious shortages of food in 1586 and from 1594 to 1598. Here is what was done in Bristol:

*Document Three*
**1586.** This year was provided by Thomas

15

Aldworth, alderman, and James Cullimore of London, haberdasher, 5 ships out of Lyn and Boston, laden with wheat, rye, malt and barley, to the value of £2600. It was brought to the City of Bristol, and did relieve Wales up Severn, and the country about us, to the great comfort of all the people.

**1596.** This year all manner of corn was dear, and Mr. John Whitsom of Bristol, merchant, brought 3000 quarters of Polish rye for this City, which rye was soon sold.

*Rikart's Kalendar*

1 What was brought to Bristol, to help prevent famine? (It was not given away, but it would have been sold cheaply.)

As you saw in the Introduction, an important way of giving charity was to build almshouses for old people. John Stow describes three groups of almshouses in London:

*Document Four*
In Woodroffe Lane are certain proper alms houses, fourteen in number, built of brick and timber, given by Sir John Milborne, draper, sometime mayor, 1521. In them he placed fourteen aged poor men and their wives, if they have wives; these have their dwellings rent free, and 2s-4d each, the first day of every month, for ever.
*A Survey of London*

Note: 2s-4d is 28 old pennies.

1 How many almshouses are there in Woodroffe Lane?
2 Who gave them? What was his occupation? What office did he hold in 1521?
3 How much money does each old person have, in old pennies? How often is it paid? How much is this, every year, in old pennies?

*Document Five*
On the east side of Monkswell Street be proper almshouses, twelve in number, given by Sir Ambrose Nicholas, salter, Mayor 1575. In them he placed twelve poor and aged people rent free, having each of them seven pence the week, and once the year each of them five sacks of coal and twenty-five faggots as his gift for ever.

*Notes:* A salter was a man who sold salt. Salt was needed to preserve food, so people bought far more than we do today.
'faggot' – bundle of firewood

1 How many almshouses are there in Monkswell Street?
2 Who founded them? What was his occupation? What office did he hold in 1575?
3 How much money does each old person have, in old pennies? How often is it paid? How much is this, every year, in old pennies?
4 What do the old people have, as well as money?

*Document Six*
On the east side of Stayning Lane be ten alms-houses, wherein be placed ten Alms people, every one of them having eight pence every Friday for ever, by the gift of Thomas Huntlow, haberdasher, one of the sheriffs in the year 1539. More, Sir George Baron later gave them £1 each by the year for ever.
*A Survey of London*

Note: £1 was 240 old pennies

1 How many almshouses are there in Stayning Lane?
2 What was the occupation of Thomas Huntlow, the man who gave them? (Look this word up in a dictionary.) What office did he hold in 1539?
3 How much money did Thomas Huntlow give the old people? How often is it paid? How much is this every year?
4 How much extra did Sir George Baron give them? How often is it paid?
5 How much do the old people have every year, in all? (Give your answer in old pennies.)

**Figure 2**  Oundle School today   Who founded this school?
(See page 15)

| Almshouses | Total money for the year (Old pennies) |
|---|---|
| Woodroffe Lane | |
| Monkswell Street | |
| Stayning Lane | |

*Documents Four – Six*

1  You can see that the men who gave the almshouses all had the same kind of occupation. What was it?

2  How can you tell they were important in the City of London?

3  There are important differences between the almshouses:

   **a.**  The old people are paid at different times. What are these times?

   **b.**  One group of old people has something in addition to money. What is that?

   **c.**  The money the old people have is not the same. Copy this table and fill it in:

One problem for most old people in almshouses was that their money remained the same, while prices went on rising. That meant they could buy less and less. Sir George Baron helped the people in Stayning Lane solve this problem. What did he do? No doubt the folk in other almshouses hoped someone would do the same for them. Whether that happened or not, was a matter of luck.

None the less, all old people in almshouses were fortunate. At least they had a home, a little money and, perhaps, a few extras like free coal and firewood.

# C   The London Hospitals

Almshouses were for people who were too old to work, but were able to look after themselves. For those who could not, or would not, do anything at all, there were hospitals. Here, we shall look at the ones in London. They were copied in towns all over the country.

## St. Bartholomew's Hospital

St. Bartholomew's Hospital was founded in 1123. With it there was a priory, which is a kind of monastery. To look after the hospital there was a Master, eight monks and four nuns. The nuns were called 'nursing sisters.' In 1537, Henry VIII dissolved the priory, and there were no more monks or nuns. As a result, the hospital could do little to help the poor. However, in 1544, the king gave it to the City of London. John Stow wrote:

*Document One*
The Bishop of Rochester, preaching at Paul's Cross, declared the gift of the king to the citizens for relieving the poor. Then, the inhabitants were all called to their parish churches. Sir Richard Dobbes, then mayor, their Aldermen, or other grave citizens told them how much good would come to them and their City, if the poor were taken from the streets and cared for in Hospitals. Therefore was every man persuaded to give what he could towards the preparing of such Hospitals, and also what they could contribute weekly towards their maintenance.
*A Survey of London*

1  How were the people told about the king's gift of the hospital?
2  Where were all the inhabitants called?
3  Who spoke to them?
4  What did they say would be the advantage of having hospitals?
5  What were the people of London persuaded to do?

St. Bartholomew's Hospital is still there today. It has different buildings, but they are on the same site, near Smithfield.

## St. Thomas's Hospital

St. Thomas's Hospital was south of the river, in Southwark, and near the end of London Bridge. Unlike St. Bartholomew's it was actually closed by Henry VIII. This was in 1540. Then, in 1551, King Edward VI gave the building to London and it was reopened in the same year. Again, the citizens gave generously:

*Document Two*
Mr. Cathrop gave 500 featherbeds and 500 straw mattresses to lay under the featherbeds, and as many blankets, and a thousand pairs of sheets. And others there were that brought featherbeds, coverlets, sheets, blankets, shirts and smocks, and gave great sums of money.
*Familiar and Friendly Discourse*, 1582, John Howe

1  What things did people give the hospital?

St. Thomas's Hospital is still in existence. In about 1870 it was moved to a new site on the side of the Thames, opposite the Houses of Parliament. The old site was used for London Bridge Station, but St. Thomas's Street still runs by the station, to remind us where the hospital once stood.

## Christ's Hospital

The people of London were particularly worried about homeless orphan children, so they decided to give them a hospital of their own. Because Henry VIII had dissolved the monasteries, numbers of them lay empty. Among them was Grey Friars, which was very near St. Bartholomew's. A few days before he died in 1553, the young King Edward VI was persuaded to give it to the citizens of London. They turned it into a children's home and called it 'Christ's Hospital.' John Howe, who was treasurer of the hospital wrote:

**Figure 1** Edward VI giving St. Thomas's Hospital its Charter.

*Document Three*
They took out of the streets all the fatherless children and other poor men's children that were not able to keep them, and brought them to the late dissolved house of Grey Friars. This they made into a hospital for them, where they should have food, drink and clothes, lodging and learning, and people to care for them.
*Familiar and Friendly Discourse*, 1582

1  What children were taken into Christ's Hospital?
2  What were they given in the hospital? (How would we say they were given 'learning'?)

John Stow wrote:
*Document Four*
In the year 1553, began the repairing of the Grey Friar's house for the poor fatherless children. And in the month of November, the children were taken into the same to the number of almost four hundred. On Christmas Day, while the Lord Mayor and Aldermen rode to St. Paul's the children of Christ's Hospital lined the street all in one livery of russet linen. And at Easter next they were in blue, and so have continued ever since.
*A Survey of London*

*Note*: 'russet' – reddish brown

1. How many children were taken into Christ's Hospital?
2. What were they made to do on Christmas Day, 1553?
3. What colour was their uniform?
4. What colour uniform were they given the following Easter?

Today, Christ's Hospital is a famous school. It moved to Horsham in Surrey in 1902, when the old site was used to build the General Post Office. The pupils still have blue uniforms, and they wear bright yellow stockings. The colour, it was thought, kept the rats from biting the children's legs.

## Bridewell Hospital

In 1553 the citizens of London asked Edward VI if they could have a disused royal palace, called Bridewell. This is part of their petition to the king:

*Document Five*
It was obvious to all men that beggars and thieves were everywhere. And we found the cause was that they were idle; and the cure must be to make them work. And all men have said to the idle, 'Work! Work!'

And we saw also that most beggars are so feared that few men dare give them work. We decided that there could be no way to help this miserable sort, but by providing work ourselves, so that the strong and sturdy vagabond may be made to earn his living. For this we need a house of work. And unto it shall be brought the sturdy and idle, and there they may be set to labour. And so, we now ask for the king's majesty's house of Bridewell. In this house shall be different occupations, wherein shall be trained all vagabonds and beggars. The weaker sort shall make feather-bed covers, draw wire, spin, knit and wind silk; and the stubborn, fouler sort, shall make nails and do other iron-work.
*Records and Court Books of Bridewell Hospital*

1. According to this petition, why do people become beggars and thieves?
2. What is the best way of curing them of being beggars and thieves?
3. Why are few men willing to employ beggars?
4. What have the citizens of London decided they must do to help beggars?
5. What building do they ask the king to give them?

**Figure 2**  Bridewell Palace, Blackfriars, where Unilever House stands today.

**6** What are the weaker beggars to do in this building?

**7** What will the worst kind of beggars be made to do?

Edward VI gave his palace of Bridewell to the citizens of London, and they did with it what they had planned. It remained a 'house of correction' where beggars and vagabonds were made to work, until 1855. It closed in that year and was demolished soon afterwards. Today, the Unilever Building stands on the site.

## Were the Hospitals a Success?

In 1587, John Howe wrote:

*Document Six*
In St. Bartholomew's Hospital there are usually 140 persons and there are cured of their diseases, one year with another 442.

In St. Thomas's Hospital there are usually 200 people and there are cured of all diseases one year with another 400 persons.

In Christ's Hospital there are usually 540 poor children and there are of them yearly preferred to sundry services and to the universities 150.
*Second Familiar and Friendly Discourse*

*Notes*:  'one year with another' – in an average year
'preferred to service' – given a job

**1** How many people are there at a time in St. Bartholomew's and St. Thomas's?

**2** How many are cured every year?

**3** Which seems the better of the two hospitals? (We would want more evidence to be sure.)

**4** How many children are there in Christ's Hospital?

**5** How many leave each year? What happens to them?

But Howe also wrote:

*Document Seven*
The streets still swarm with beggars. No man can stand in any street, but at once ten or twelve beggars come breathing in his face. Many of them have plague sores and other contagious diseases running on them, wandering from man to man to seek money. This is very dangerous to all her majesty's good subjects, and very likely to infect the whole kingdom.
*Second Familiar and Friendly Discourse*

**1** According to Howe, how many beggars are likely to approach anyone who goes into the street?

**2** Why are these beggars dangerous?

Howe explains why there are so many beggars in London:

*Document Eight*
It is not the poor of London that pester the City, but the poor of England. London draws to itself all soldiers who have no wars to employ them, and all wounded soldiers come to London to be cured. All serving men whose masters are dead come to London to find new masters. All masterless men, whose masters have cast them off for some offence or other, come to London to find work. There is also a number of idle people, as lusty rogues and common beggars, who are neither soldiers nor serving men. But hearing of the great generosity of London, they come here for money. These are the caterpillars of our country, and not belonging here, are the people which overcharge London, and are those that give the City such a bad name.
*Second Familiar and Friendly Discourse*

**1** Why do soldiers come to London?

**2** Why are there many serving men out of work?

**3** Why do they come to London?

**4** Why do many rogues and beggars come to London?

As you can see, Howe says that most of the beggars in London did not belong there, but came from the rest of England. He felt that London could look after its own poor, but not all the outsiders that came there.

# D   The Beggars of Norwich

In many towns there were large numbers of beggars. Here is a report from Norwich:

*Document One*
Many of the citizens were annoyed that the city was so full with poor people, both men, women and children, to the number of 2300 persons, who went from door to door begging, pretending a kind of work, but did very little or none. Moreover, they were not content to take at men's doors only what they needed, but having eaten too much, they cast the rest into the street. They might be followed by the trail of pottage, bread, meat and drink which they spoiled. These crews did not trouble to find lodgings, but used church porches, cellars, doorways, barns, hay lofts and other back corners. Some as had houses lay upon the cold ground. So cared they not for clothing, though the cold struck so deep into them, that what with diseases and want of care, their flesh was eaten with vermin and bad diseases grew upon them so fast that they were past cure. More-over, the ale houses were stuffed with gamblers and drunkards that so tended the drink all day that they could not incline to work. And in their pots they abused the holy name of God with swearing, prating and lying, and defiled their bodies with filthiness.
*Records of the City of Norwich, 1571*

1   How many beggars were there in Norwich?
2   What did they do with much of the food they were given?
3   Where did many of them sleep?
4   Why were they often cold?
5   The report says they did not take proper care of themselves. What was wrong with them, as a result?
6   What were some of the things they did in the ale houses?

Here are some orders the Town Council made to deal with beggars:

*Document Two*
**None to beg in pain of six stripes**
No person shall beg at any place within the City in pain of six stripes with a whip.

**None to sustain any beggars at their doors**
No person or persons shall help or feed any beggars in pain of a fine of four pence.

**A working place at the Normans for men and women**
At the house called the Normans there shall be a working place for men and women. For the men there are to be malt querns to grind malt and such exercises. And for the women to spin and card and such like exercises.

**Twelve persons to be set to work**
Which working place shall set twelve persons upon work, which persons shall be kept as prisoners to work for meat and drink for twenty and one days at least. They shall not eat but as they can earn. Such persons as shall be sent thither, shall be such as be able to work, but will not work, but rather beg, or else be vagabonds or idlers. Those that refuse to do their work to be punished by the whip.
*Orders for the Poor, Norwich, 1571*

**Figure 1**   Beggar

**Figure 2** Preparing Wool for Spinning This is the kind of work women had to do in the Norwich Bridewell.

*Notes*: 'Normans' – a big, old house in Norwich
'quern' – device for grinding corn. Using it was hard work, for it meant turning a heavy stone by hand.
'carding' – preparing wool for spinning

1　What is to happen to anyone caught begging in Norwich?
2　What is to happen to anyone who helps a beggar?
3　What work is to be done at the Normans?
4　What people are to be sent there?
5　What will happen to anyone who refuses to work?

There were many children and young people in Norwich who were beggars. The Town Council did not send them to the Normans. It allowed them to eat and sleep at home, but it paid a number of women to look after them during the day. These women had to be chosen with care, so they were known as the 'select women.' Here is what they were supposed to do:

### Document Three

You are to receive every working day into your home, six, eight, ten or twelve of such idle young persons that run about begging.

To these you are to do your good will in teaching them, but especially to compel them to work. And if they will not work, to give punishment, six stripes with a rod.
*Orders for the Select Women*, Norwich 1571

1　How many young people does each of the select women look after?
2　What must the young people do?
3　What will happen if they refuse?

This is what happened in Norwich after the new rules had been made:

### Document Four

These orders have been tried and found to have these good results.

First, that of 950 children which daily was idle and did nothing but beg, the same now kept at work may earn, one with another, sixpence a week.

Also that 64 men which daily did beg and lived idly now do earn twelve pence a week at the least.

Also that 180 women which daily did beg and lived idly are now able to earn at least twelve pence, some twenty pence, some thirty pence a week.

Besides, the magistrates are not now troubled with the tenth part of the vagabonds, for fear of the terror of the work house.
*Records of the City of Norwich*, 1571

1　How many children, men and women in Norwich are now working instead of begging? How many is that in all?
2　How many people have been unable to find work? (Look back to Document One to see how many beggars there had been.)
3　Why are fewer vagabonds being brought before the magistrates?

# 3  Care of the Poor in Ipswich

## A  Introduction

Ipswich is a town that takes good care of its poor people. We will ask one of its citizens, Thomas Kenington, to explain what is done.

'*What do you do for the poor people in your town?*'

'A great deal. We have the Tooley Foundation, we have Christ's Hospital, and we have outdoor relief.'

'*What is the Tooley Foundation?*'

'It is named after Henry Tooley. He was one of our richest merchants. He had no children and when he died in 1551 he left almost everything he owned to the poor of Ipswich. Nearly all his wealth was in land and houses. Four of the leading citizens now look after this property. They let it out and they use the rents to help the poor.'

'*How is that done?*'

'In his will, Henry Tooley said there were to be five almshouses, each for two old people. When the almshouses were built, it was found that there was still plenty of money left. As a result, the Foundation took over part of an old monastery and made it into more homes for old people. The Foundation now cares for no less than forty folk who are too old to work. They must count themselves lucky. They have somewhere to live, they have fuel, they have clothing, and they have pensions. The pension is usually a shilling a week. It is not much, but it will buy enough food for one old person.'

'*Who started Christ's Hospital?*'

'The Town Council did, in 1568. It saw that the Tooley Foundation was not enough, so it opened a poor house of its own.'

'*Where is it?*'

'In another part of the old monastery used by the Tooley Foundation.'

'*That old monastery has proved very useful!*'

'Certainly it is more useful now than when it was full of fat, idle monks.'

'*Does Christ's Hospital care for people who are ill?*'

'Yes, it has a sick room. But most of the folk in the Hospital are well enough. It is just that they cannot, or will not, look after themselves. Some are unable to do so because they are lame or blind. Some are too old. Some are orphan children. There are also a few who could quite well earn their own living, but are just lazy. We shut them up and give them jobs like spinning and weaving and making candles.'

'*What happens if they still refuse to work?*'

'They don't eat.'

'*You mentioned outdoor relief. What is that?*'

'Let me first explain indoor relief. That is taking people into places like the Tooley Foundation and Christ's Hospital. Outdoor relief, on the other hand, is giving money to people who remain in their own homes.'

'*What kind of people are they?*'

'Good, hard-working folk, for the most part. But try as they may, they cannot earn all the money they need. Some are men with large families. Some are poor widows with children. But they can do a lot for themselves. With a few pence in outdoor relief, they manage quite well.'

'*How do you find all the money you need for the poor?*'

'As I explained, the Tooley Foundation has the rents from the land and houses it owns. The money for Christ's Hospital, and all the money for the outdoor relief, comes from the general collection.'

'*What is that?*'

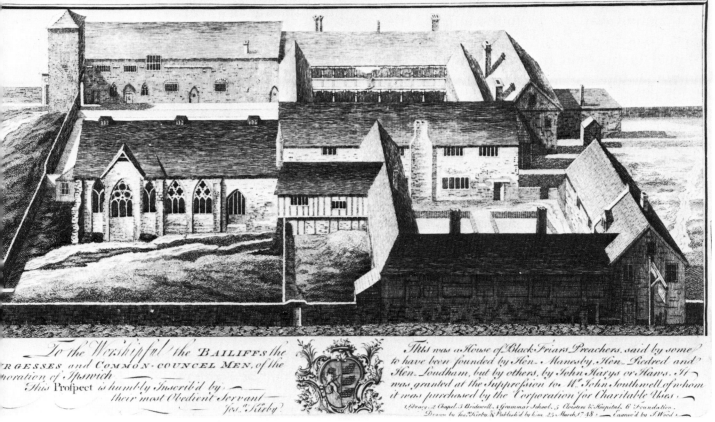

THE WEST VIEW OF CHRIST'S HOSPITAL IN IPSWICH.

**Figure 1** Priory of Blackfriars, Ipswich.

'People who own houses or land have to pay a certain amount each week. The money is then given to the poor. I am an overseer of the poor. That means I am one of the men who makes sure the system works properly. It is a thankless task. Everyone who pays is sure he is being made to give too much. At the same time, everyone who has relief is sure he receives too little. I remind them of the time when the town swarmed with beggars, but they still grumble.'

1  How did the Tooley Foundation get its name?

2  How does it find money to help the poor?

3  Name two sets of homes which the Tooley Foundation has for poor people.

4  What poor people does the Tooley Foundation help?

5  What does the Foundation give them?

6  Who started Christ's Hospital? Where is it?

7  What are the people in Christ's Hospital unable to do? Give some of the reasons for this.

8  What jobs are given to lazy people?

9  What happens if they refuse to do them?

10  What is outdoor relief?

11  Give some examples of people who receive it.

12  Who pays money into the general collection?

13  How is the money spent?

# B  The Tooley Foundation

As you saw in the introduction, the Tooley Foundation was run by four wardens. They met from time to time to decide what they should do to help the poor people in the town. They wrote down what they agreed in a book. Here are some extracts from it:

*Document One*
It is ordered and agreed by the wardens of Mr. Tooley's Foundation that Alice Taylor, an aged and impotent wench of this town, in respect of her poverty, age and lameness shall be admitted to the said Foundation, and that she shall have allowed to her 6d. a week for her relief.

It is agreed that John Wiseman and Agnes his wife, being two old, aged and impotent people of this town who have been inhabitants in the same by the space of 30 years and more, and of honest fame and report, shall in respect of their ages and poverty be placed in one of the houses of Mr. Tooley's Foundation.

It is ordered that Joan Carre and Em Partriche, two old women of the Foundation who now lie sick, that both of them shall have two pence increase of their former reliefs for as long as they shall be ill.

It is ordered that Helen Hadnam an old, poor woman of the Foundation, in consideration that she is now blind and thereby unable to earn anything, that she shall have two pence of increase to be added to her former relief of 10d.

It is agreed that Agnes Thunder shall have 2s-0d allowed her towards the charge of the healing of her mouth.
*Ordinances of the Tooley Foundation, 1588–9*

*Notes:*   'impotent' – helpless
'admitted to the Foundation' – given a home belonging to the Foundation
'relief' – money given every week, like a pension

1  Why did the wardens decide to give Alice Taylor a home?
2  How much money was she to have?
3  Why did the wardens decide to give John and Agnes Wiseman a home?
4  Why did the wardens decide to give extra money to **a** Joan Carre and Em Partriche **b** Helen Hadnam?

**Figure 1**   The Tooley Brass   This is a memorial to Henry Tooley. It was once in the church of St. Mary Quay, Ipswich.

henricus Toolye obიit
rrii° Augusti A° 1551.
Allicia Toolye obიit დიი
die ffebruarū A° 1565.

**Figure 2**  *The Parable of the Blind*  This painting by Brueghel shows the misery of folk who were both poor and blind. It was people like this that the Tooley Foundation tried to help.

**5** Why was Agnes Thunder given money?

**6** Judging by these extracts, what kind of people did the wardens of the Tooley Foundation try to help?

Here now are some of the payments which the wardens made in 1588:

*Document Two*

| | |
|---|---|
| Paid to Edward Newman, one poor person of the Foundation towards his relief for 52 weeks at 12d the week | 52s-0d |
| Paid to Eleanor Thompson, one poor person of the Foundation, for 52 weeks at 8d the week (There are 36 entries like these two.) | 34s-8d |
| Paid to Mother Harrison and Mother Taylor, being sick at different times | 1s-4d |
| Paid for a waistcoat for Mother White and one pair of hose for Mother Harrison, with making of both | 3s-5d |
| Paid to Mistress Gilbert for $8\frac{3}{4}$ yards of kersey to make hose, at $22\frac{1}{2}$d the yard | 26s-0$\frac{1}{2}$d |
| Paid to Thomas Borrow for shoes | 30s-4d |
| Paid to the churchwardens of St. Mary-on-the-Quay for one whole year | 10s-0d |

| | |
|---|---|
| Paid for 52$\frac{1}{4}$ ells of canvas at 11d the ell which made sheets, shirts and smocks | 46s-11d |
| Paid for making 19 smocks, 4 shirts and 3 pairs of sheets | 5s-8d |
| Paid to Mistress Gilbert for 2$\frac{1}{2}$ yards of whited canvas and is for a sheet to bury Isabel Huntick | 2s-6d |
| Paid for the funeral charges of Isabel Huntick | 1s-8d |
| Paid to Peter, a surgeon, towards the healing of Judith White's leg | 14s-4d |
| Paid for 50 loads of firewood at 4s-2d the load | £60-8s-4d |

*Ordinances of the Tooley Foundation, 1588−9*

*Notes:*  The sheet for Isabel Huntick was a winding sheet. Poor people were buried in winding sheets to save the expense of coffins. The ten shillings given to the churchwardens were to pay for seats for the poor people in the church. Church seating was not free in the sixteenth century, as it is today.
'kersey' – kind of woollen cloth
'ell' – 45 inches (114 centimetres)

**1** How many people had pensions from the Tooley Foundation?

**2** Make a list of all the other ways in which the wardens of the Tooley Foundation helped the poor.

# C Christ's Hospital

As you saw in the introduction, Christ's Hospital belonged to the Town Council. It did not have its own, separate, building, but shared the old monastery of Blackfriars with the Tooley Foundation.

We know something about the people who were in Christ's Hospital from a register that was kept. On the left hand pages of the register a clerk wrote the names of the folk who came into the Hospital, and a few facts about them. Opposite, on the right hand pages, he said what happened to them in the end.

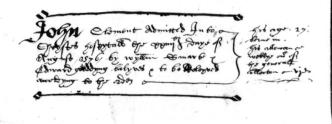 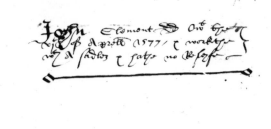

Here are some entries from the register:

**Figure 1**  Part of the Register of Christ's Hospital

*Document One*

| | |
|---|---|
| Alice Barnes, widow, admitted to Christ's Hospital the 23rd day of December 1569. Her age 60 years. Her allowance 12d weekly. | Alice Barnes departed this life the 26th day of May 1577 and is buried in the churchyard of St. Mary Quay. |
| Rose Bennes, a single woman, admitted into Christ's Hospital the 14th day of May 1573. Her age 50 years. Her allowance out of the weekly general collection 7d. | Rose Bennes delivered out the 29th day of May 1574, and placed in the foundation of Mr. Tooley's in the room of Mother London. |
| Annes Jolly, widow, admitted into Christ's Hospital the 17th day of July 1573. Her age 96 years. Her allowance weekly from the general collection 12d. | Annes Jolly delivered out the 22nd of January 1574, and her son Thomas Jolly to keep her, having 12d the week |
| Henry Southern admitted into Christ's Hospital the 29th day of January 1573, having a very sore leg. His allowance 12d weekly. His age 26 years. | Henry Southern delivered out the 5th of March 1576, and is married to Katherine Moore. |
| Henry Taylor admitted into Christ's Hospital the 15th day of August 1574 and being sick to stay till he be well. His age 38. His allowance 12d a week. | Henry Taylor delivered out the 6th day of September 1574 and having a passport to go to the coast on fishing. |
| Jane Booth, a wayfaring woman, sent to the Hospital the 5th of February 1575 by Thomas Blosse, one of the constables, for one night's lodging, food and drink. | Jane Booth went from the Hospital the 6th of February 1575, having a passport to travel to London. Chargeable to the house: one supper and breakfast. |
| John Clement admitted into Christ's Hospital the 24th day of August 1576. His age 27. His allowance weekly out of the general collection, 6d. | John Clement departed out the 6th of April 1577 and worketh with a sadler and hath no relief. |
| Christopher Long committed to the Hospital the 7th day of September 1577, and there to be punished for running away from his master, dwelling in London. His age 19 years. Born in Cornwall. | Christopher Long delivered the 7th of September 1577, and sent to London by a passport, having the whipping almost. |
| Sybil Palmer, and her son, a child of the age of 4 years, sent to the Hospital the 25th day of March 1579, and there to be relieved according to the order of strangers coming to the town. She is seeking for her husband, William Palmer. | Sybil Palmer delivered the 27th day of March with her child, and a passport from the town, and her time to be at London by Easter next, she lodging in the Hospital two nights and four meals. |

*Register of Christ's Hospital*

'general collection' – money the richer people in the town had to pay for the poor

'delivered out' – sent away, or left

'passport' – written permission from a magistrate to travel about the country. No poor person was allowed to travel without a passport.

'wayfaring woman' – female tramp

1  How old was Alice Barnes when she came into the hospital? How much money was she allowed? How long did she stay in the hospital? What happened to her, in the end?

2  How old was Rose Bennes when she came into the hospital? What happened to her?

3  Why did Annes Jolly leave the hospital? What help was she given, after she left?

4  How old was Henry Southern, when he came into the hospital? Why did he come into the hospital? How long did he stay? What happened to him when he left?

5  Why did Henry Taylor come into the hospital? How long did he stay? What happened to him when he left?

6  Who was Jane Booth? Why did she come into the hospital? How long did she stay?

7  How old was John Clement? How long did he stay in the hospital? What happened to him when he left?

8  Why was Christopher Long sent to the hospital? How long did he stay? What happened to him?

9  Why was Sybil Palmer travelling round the country? Who was with her? How long did she stay in the hospital? What was she told to do when she left?

10  How was a sixteenth century hospital different from a modern one?

Document Two shows some of the expenses of Christ's Hospital:

## Document Two

| | |
|---|---|
| Paid to Thomas Borrow for 27 pairs of shoes for the poor in the hospital | £1-6s-4d |
| Paid at London for 67 ells of canvas and for bringing it home at 11d per ell to make shirts and smocks | £3-3s-10d |
| Paid to Mother Johnson for 28 pairs of knit hose | 17s-0d |
| Paid for making 46 shirts and smocks and for thread; and for 18 coifs and a kercher; and for 20 aprons | 9s-10d |
| Paid to Lawrence Bodnam for 60 loads of wood at 4s-0d per load | £12-0s-0d |
| Paid to Ralph Canaway for mending of shoes | £1-9s-0d |
| Paid for 6 bushels of rye | £2-8s-0d |
| Paid to Bartholemew Fenne for two bushels of peas for porridge | 4s-0d |
| Paid to John Minter for making an overbody and mending a petticoat of Madeleine Harrison | 4d |
| Paid for the burial of Nicholas Smith, a poor child at the hospital | 8d |
| Paid to Warren Hadley for 6 pairs of cards | 6s-0d |
| Paid to Robert Kennington for divers cures done on the poor children in the hospital | £2-6s-2d |
| For 8 dozen tin buttons for the boys' cotes | 1s-4d |
| For half an ell of canvas for an upper body for one of the great wenches and to line her waistcoat | 7d |
| In hooks and eyes for a waistcoat | $\frac{1}{2}$d |

*(There are also weekly payments to 35 people in the hospital. Most of them had 10d or 12d each.) Accounts of Christ's Hospital*

Notes:  'ell' – 45 inches (114 cm.)

'coif' – close fitting cap, usually worn by old people

'kercher' – head scarf

'bushel' – measure of grain. About 36 litres.

'porridge'– soup

'cards' – tools used to prepare wool for spinning

1  These expenses tell us some of the things which were done for the poor in Christ's Hospital. What were they?

2  Compare the expenses of Christ's Hospital with those of the Tooley Foundation. Are they much the same, or quite different?

3  Note the 'peas for porridge'. Probably, you know a nursery rhyme about 'peas porridge'. What is it?

## D Outdoor Relief

The Tooley Foundation and Christ's Hospital were for people who were too old or too ill to look after themselves, and had no-one to care for them. There were plenty of poor people, though, who could go on living in their own homes, if only they were given a little money. At one time they had gone begging, but in 1572 Parliament made a law saying that every parish must look after it own poor. A parish is an area served by a church. In the countryside it is usually the same as a village. A town is divided into a number of parishes.

Under the new law, the richer people in every parish had to pay a certain amount each week, and this money was given to the poor. Here are some lists from St. Margaret's parish, Ipswich:

*Document One*
The rate taxed of inhabitants the 25th day of August in the 16th year of the reign of our Sovereign Lady the Queen for the weekly charge towards the relief of the poor by John Moore, William Smart and Robert Sparrow, justices.

| | |
|---|---|
| Edmund Wythepoll Esq. | 16d |
| Dame Margaret Jermye | 4d |
| Robert Ball, gentleman | 2d |
| John Brenne | 4d |
| William Lymfeld | 4d |
| John Cole | 6d |
| John Gardner | 4d |
| Robert Hall | 3d |
| Thomas Cock | 1d |
| Lawrence Bodnam | 2d |
| Richard Bennett | 1d |
| Thomas Hoodles | 1d |
| William Johnson | 2d |
| Edward Ballard | 2d |
| Robert Bennes | 1d |
| John Withey | 1d |
| John Ropkin | 1d |
| Thomas Whitman | 1d |
| Mrs. Rysbye | 6d |
| John Cockock | 1d |
| Jasper Meremounte | 1d |
| Thomas Kenington | 1d |
| Jasper Bayly | 1d |

**Figure 1** Sixteenth Century Houses in Ipswich   The wealthy people, who paid money to help the poor, lived in houses like this.

| | | | |
|---|---|---|---|
| Roger Barnye | 3d | Widow Skinner | 4d |
| Mr. Leche | 4d | Widow Cockshedge | 4d |
| James Thompson | 1d | Robert Dameron | 3d |
| Nicholas Norton | 1d | Widow Thompson | 2d |
| John Dawson | 1d | William Stiver | 2d |
| Peter Cole | 2d | Edward Newman | 4d |
| Michael Lytleburie | 1d | Henry Poynard | 2d |
| Robert Dawes | 1d | William Thonnelles | 4d |
| Humphrey Harman gent. | 4d | Widow Sudbury | 4d |
| Robert Hynes | 1d | Reinolde's child | 12d |
| John Pretyman | 3d | Widow Barker | 8d |
| William Medowe | 1d | Thomas Harpan | 4d |
| Alice Ryvett, widow | 2d | Widow Byet | 4d |
| John Gibbon, gent. | 3d | Widow Saunder | 3d |

| | |
|---|---|
| Widow Butler | 3d |
| A lame wench at Orgon's | 2d |
| Tyse's wife for keeping a child | 9d |
| To Field for keeping of Austen | 4d |
| To Water's wife for keeping of Bettes | 6d |

Collectors    John Gardner, tanner, and Thomas Cock
Overseer    Thomas Kenington

*Assessments, St. Margaret's, Ipswich 1574*

*Weekly Payments to the Poor, St. Margaret's, Ipswich, 1574*

*Notes:*    The overseer said how much everyone should pay, and the justices, that is the magistrates, decided whether he had been fair. What was the work of the collectors, do you suppose?

You can see that the names of the two collectors and the overseer are on the list of assessments. They were ordinary men who did these jobs in their spare time, for nothing. They changed every year, all the ratepayers taking their turn.

1    What was the largest amount anyone paid in poor rates?
2    What was the smallest amount?
3    Draw up a table to show how many people paid 1d, how many 2d, how many 3d, and so on.

Here now is a list which shows how much each poor person received:

*Document Two*

| | |
|---|---|
| Margaret Estall, widow | 4d |
| Mother Orgon | 4d |
| Widow Dameron | 4d |
| Richard Kirk | 3d |
| Mother Collen | 6d |
| Widow Butler | 3d |
| William Deye | 4d |

*Note:*    Some of the people did not need money for themselves, but were being paid to look after others who needed care. Reinolde's child must have had something seriously wrong with it. The parents needed the money, perhaps for medicine and doctor's fees, perhaps for special food.

If you add up the two lists you will find that more was paid out than was collected. The difference was made up by other parishes in the town which did not have so many poor people.

1    What was the largest amount of money that was given away each week?
2    What was the smallest amount?
3    Apart from the largest one, how do these amounts compare with the sums paid to people in the Tooley Foundation and Christ's Hospital? How do you explain the difference? (See what is said about outdoor relief in the *Introduction*.)
4    Draw up a table to show how many people had 2d, how many 3d, how many 4d, and so on.

# 4 Vagabonds

## A Introduction

It is 1600. We will ask a magistrate to tell us about vagabonds. His name is Edward Hext, and he lives in Somerset.

*'What is a vagabond?'*

'He is someone who refuses to live in one place and work for his living. Instead, he wanders about the countryside begging, stealing and robbing.'

*'Why do people become vagabonds?'*

'Most of them do so because they like an idle, roving life better than working. However, there are some who become vagabonds unwillingly enough. In certain parts of England the farmers have more workers than they need. They give numbers of them the sack and these unhappy men turn to begging.

More seriously, we have just had several wars. The Queen sent armies into Ireland, the Low Countries and France. When the soldiers returned, too little was done for them. They were just dismissed, and had to look after themselves. Such men are dangerous. They have had an exciting time in the army, so they are unwilling to settle down to dull, boring jobs. Also, many of them are young, strong and brave. They will commit any crime, rather than go hungry. The worst time was in 1589. Sir Francis Drake and Sir John Norreys invaded Portugal and when they returned their men were sent away with just five shillings each. They were furious, and gangs of them gathered near London. A mob of 500 threatened to loot Bartholomew Fair. The Lord Mayor had to call out the Trained Bands to restore order. The people of London were prepared to fight the Spaniards, if they landed, but they hardly expected an attack from an English army.'

*'Vagabonds seem a serious problem.'*

'They are the worst problem we have. For one thing, there are so many of them. They are as difficult to count as stray cats, but I think there are at least three or four hundred in every county. Also, the people they hurt most are the poor. A rich man has servants to guard his property. The poor man must try to watch his house, his crops, his animals and his poultry, all on his own. This, of course, he cannot do, and so he is robbed. I questioned a rogue only the other day who said that he and two others had stayed with a dishonest inn-keeper for three weeks. During that time they had stolen and eaten a sheep every day. Such villains will even take a farmer's ox. That means he is ruined, for he has no animal to pull his plough.

Vagabonds also spread terror. You can imagine how a woman feels, when her man is out working, and two or three sturdy villains come to her door. At first they will whine and beg, but as soon as they realise the woman is alone they make threats. They will not leave her until she has given them money and all the food and drink they want. Worse than that can happen. There is a lonely farm some miles from here where vagabonds come and go as they please. They will enter the house uninvited and without even knocking, and sit down by the fire, or join the family for a meal. The farmer tells me he sometimes has as many as thirty at a time sleeping in his barn. He dare not refuse them for fear of being killed or having his house burnt to the ground.'

*'What do you do about vagabonds?'*

'Any we take are given a good whipping and sent back to the place where they were born. The people there are supposed to set

**Figure 1**  Beggars, an etching by Rembrandt

**Figure 2**  Beggar

them to work. But true vagabonds will gladly risk a whipping rather than stay at home for long. Sooner or later, off they go again, plaguing the countryside like a swarm of caterpillars.

We are at war with Spain, and we are likely to be invaded. I am sure, though, that our own English vagabonds are more dangerous enemies than all of King Philip's soldiers.'

*Notes:*  'Trained Bands' – London's army of part-time soldiers. All the citizens had to do some military training for a few days every year, and could be called on to defend the city if it was in danger.

Sixteenth century sheep were quite small, and three men could easily eat one in a day.

1 What are vagabonds?
2 According to Hext, what is the main reason people become vagabonds?
3 Name two groups of people who become vagabonds unwillingly.
4 Why are vagabonds difficult to count, do you suppose?
5 How many vagabonds does Hext think there are in every county?
6 Which people do vagabonds harm the most?
7 In what ways do vagabonds make trouble?
8 What happens to any vagabonds that are caught?
9 Does this stop people being vagabonds?

## B  Why People became Vagabonds

For much of the sixteenth century, wool fetched a good price, so, in some parts of England the landowners and richer farmers grew less corn and kept more sheep. That meant they turned much of their ploughed land into grass land. As a result, they needed fewer workers. Instead of large numbers of people doing all the tasks of ploughing, harrowing, sowing, reaping and threshing, there were just a few shepherds. Heartless employers just sacked the men and women they did not need, and turned them out of their homes. Sir Thomas More described what was happening in his book *Utopia*:

*Document One*
Your, sheep, that used to be so meek and tame, have become so great devourers and so wild that they eat up and swallow down the very men themselves. For look in what parts of the realm doth grow the finest and therefore dearest wool, there noblemen and gentlemen leave no ground for tillage, but enclose all into pasture; they throw down houses, they pluck down towns, and leave nothing standing, but only the church to be made into a sheephouse. The husbandmen be thrown out of their homes. They must needs depart away, poor, wretched souls, men, women, husbands, wives, fatherless children, widows, woeful mothers, with their young babes. Away they trudge, out of their houses, finding no place to rest in. All their household goods, which are very little worth, they sell for almost nothing. And when they have wandered about till that be spent, what can they do, but steal, and be hanged, or else go begging? And yet then also they be cast in prison as vagabonds, because they go about and work not; to whom no man gives work, though they are very willing to take it.
*Utopia*

*Notes*:  'tillage' – ploughed land
　　　　'towns' – here means villages
　　　　'pasture' – grass land
　　　　'husbandman' – farm worker

1  What changes are nobles and gentlemen making in farming?
2  What do they do to houses and villages?
3  What do they do to churches?
4  What happens to the farm workers? Who suffers with them?
5  What do they do with their household goods?
6  What do they do when they have no money left?
7  According to More, are they willing to work, given the chance?

This is part of a letter which Edward Hext wrote about vagabonds:

*Document Two*
They will risk their lives rather than work. And I know this to be true, for when I sent wandering persons to the house of correction, all would beg me with bitter tears to send them rather to gaol. When I refused, some confessed felonies to me, by which they risked their lives, so they would not be sent to the house of correction where they would be made to work.
*Letter to Lord Burghley*, 1596

*Notes*:  A house of correction was a prison specially for vagabonds, and where they were made to work. In an ordinary gaol, on the other hand, the criminals did not have to do anything.
　　　　'felony' – crime for which the punishment might be hanging

1  According to Hext, how do vagabonds feel about work?
2  Why would they rather go to prison than the house of correction?
3  How would they risk their lives, in order to go to prison?
4  How does Hext disagree with More?

Here, then we have two different ideas about vagabonds, the one given by More, and the other given by Hext. When you have finished the whole of the chapter you should try to decide which is right.

# C  Different Kinds of Vagabonds

According to some sixteenth century writers, there were over twenty different kinds of vagabonds. We will look at a few of them.

## Upright Men

These were the leaders of the vagabonds, for they were the strongest and the most daring. They terrorised other vagabonds and honest people alike. Often, they did not beg for money, but demanded it. One of their stories was that they were soldiers who had fought for the Queen and been discharged without pay. Sometimes that was indeed true. Here is a description of upright men:

*Document One*
The Upright Man is one that carries a truncheon of a staff, which staff they call a 'filchman.' This man is of so much authority that, meeting with any other beggars, he may take a share or 'snap' of all that they have got by their begging. And if he do them wrong, they have no remedy against him – no, even though he beat them, as he often does.
*The Fraternity of Vagabonds*, John Awdeley

**Figure 1**  An Upright Man

1  What does the upright man carry?
2  What does he do to other beggars?

Here is Thomas Harman's description of upright men:

*Document Two*
Of these rascals, some be serving men, some town workers and some farm labourers. These, not minding to get their living by the sweat of their face, will wander through most parts of this realm. Yea, not without punishment by stocks, whippings and imprisonment. Yet they have so good liking for this kind of life that full quickly all their punishment is forgotten. And they never think of repenting until they climb three trees with a ladder.

These rascals travel in groups. If they call at a poor husbandman's house, he will go alone, or one with him, and stoutly demand his charity, either showing how he has served in the wars and there maimed, or that he seeks work. If they ask at a stout yeoman's house, they will go three or four in a company; where, for fear more than good will, they often have relief.

If he sees young pigs or poultry, he well notes the place, and shortly after, he will be sure to have some of them, which they bring to their boozing kens.
*A Caveat for Common Cursitors*

*Notes:*  'three trees with a ladder' – gallows
'husbandman' – peasant
'yeoman' – rich farmer
'relief' – money or food given to a poor man
'boozing ken' – ale house (thieves' slang)

1  What are upright men unwilling to do? (What does Harman mean by 'the sweat of their face'?)
2  How are upright men punished?
3  Do the punishments make them change their ways?
4  How many will call at a peasant's house?
5  What excuses do they make for begging?
6  How many will go to a rich farmer's house?
7  Why do the people help them?
8  What do upright men steal from farmers?

Harman also wrote:

*Document Three*
If an upright man meets any beggar, he will ask him if he was stalled to the rogue or no. If not, he will take his money, or his best garment and have him to the boozing ken, and orders him to sell the best thing he has for twenty pence or two shillings. Then the upright man calls for a quart of drink and pours the same upon his head, saying, 'I, G.P. do stall thee, W.T. to the rogue, and from now on it shall be lawful for thee to beg for thy living in all places.' Here you shall see that the upright man is of great authority. For all sorts of beggars obey him.
*A Caveat for Common Cursitors*

*Note*: 'stalled to the rogue' – made a beggar, by a special ceremony

1  You recently became a vagabond. Describe what happened when you first met an upright man.

There are no good pictures of upright men, so books usually show the one illustrated on page 35.

1  How can you tell this is not an English print?
2  Does the picture fit the descriptions of upright men given by Awdeley and Harman? (Do you think other beggars would be frightened of this man?)
3  Did beggars carry flags, do you suppose?

## Palliards

A palliard was a beggar who had dreadful sores. He hoped the sores would make people sorry for him and give him money. Often, the palliard's sores were because of disease, but not always. Thomas Dekker wrote:

*Document Four*
They take crowfoot, spearwort and salt, and, pounding them together, they lay them upon the part of the body which they desire to make sore. The skin by this means being irritated, they first clasp a linen cloth, till it stick fast, which plucked off, the raw flesh has ratsbane thrown upon it to make it look ugly. Then they cast over that a cloth, which is always bloody and filthy; which they do so often, that in the end they feel no pain, nor do they want to have it healed. With their doxies they will travel from fair to fair and from market to market. They are able by their begging to get five shillings in a week in money and corn. Which money they hide under blue and green patches. Sometimes they have about them six or seven pound together.
*O Per Se O*

*Notes*: 'crowfoot' and 'spearwort' – plants
'ratsbane' – rat poison
'doxy' – beggar woman

1  How do palliards irritate their skin?
2  Why do they stick a piece of cloth to it?
3  How do they make the sore look even worse?
4  How much money will a beggar take in a week? How much may he have hidden?

Here is a picture of a palliard:

**Figure 2**   Palliard

1  Why is the man holding up his leg, do you suppose?
2  Why does he have a bowl?

# Dummerers

Dummerers tried to make people sorry for them by pretending to be deaf and dumb. The magistrate Thomas Harman once caught a dummerer. He was sure the man was a fraud, so he was determined to make him speak. He asked a surgeon to help him and this is what happened:

*Document Five*
The surgeon made him gape and we could see but half a tongue. I told the surgeon to put his finger in his mouth and to pull out his tongue, and so he did, even though he held strongly a good while. At length he plucked out the tongue, to the great surprise of many that stood by. Yet even when we saw his tongue, he would neither speak nor yet would hear. Said I to the surgeon, 'Tie two of his fingers together, and thrust a stick between them and rub it up and down a little while and he will speak by and by.'

'Sir,' said the surgeon, 'I pray you let me try another way.'

I was well contented to see the same. He had him into a house, and tied a rope about his wrists and hoisted him over a beam, and there did let him hang a good while. At last, for very pain, he asked for God's sake to let him down. So he that was both deaf and dumb could in a short time both hear and speak. Then I took the money I found in his purse and gave the same to the poor, which was fifteen pence. That done, I sent him to the next Justice where he was put in the Pillory and was well whipped.
*A Caveat for Common Cursitors*

1 What had the dummerer done with his tongue?
2 What did the surgeon do with the tongue?
3 How did the surgeon make the dummerer speak?
4 What did Harman do with the dummerer's money?
5 How much money was there? Compare this with the amounts Dekker says beggars carried. (Page 36.)
6 How was the dummerer punished?
7 What does this extract tell you about the treatment of suspects in Elizabethan times?

# Abram Men

Abram men pretended to be mad. Thomas Dekker describes them:

*Document Six*
The abram man is a lusty, strong rogue, who walks with a sheet about his body. Often he goes without breeches; a torn jerkin, with hanging sleeves; no shirt; his face staring; his hair long and filthily knotted; a good staff in his hand, and sometimes a stick on which he hangs bacon. These, walking up and down the country, are more terrible to women and children than the name of Raw-head, Bloody-bones, Robin Goodfellow, or any other hob-goblin, so that when they come to any door begging, nothing is denied them.

To seem mad, some make a horrid noise, hollowly sounding; some whoop, some bellow, some show only a kind of wild, distracted look, begging in a mad way, with the addition of these words, 'well and wisely'. Some dance, but keep no time. Others leap up and down. There begging is thus:

'Now, dame, well and wisely, what will you give poor Tom now? One pound of your sheep's feathers to make poor Tom a blanket? Or one piece of your sow's side no bigger than my arm? Or one piece of your salt meat? Or one cross of your small silver towards buying poor Tom a pair of shoes? Ah, God bless my poor dame, well and wisely, give poor Tom an old sheet to keep him from the cold, or an old doublet of my master's. God save his life.' Then will he dance and sing, or use some other antic ending with, 'Good dame, give poor Tom one cup of the best drink – well and wisely. God save the Queen and her Council, and the governor of this place.'
*O Per Se O*

1 What clothes does the abram man wear?
2 What do abram men carry?
3 Who is particularly frightened of them?
4 What do they do to seem mad?
5 What things do they beg?

## Women vagabonds

A woman vagabond was called a 'doxy' or a 'mort'. Thomas Dekker describes a typical doxy:

*Document Seven*
On her back she carries a great pack in which she carries all the things she steals. Her skill sometimes is to tell fortunes, or to help the diseases of women and children. As she walks, she knits, and wears in her hat a needle with a thread in it. An excellent angler she is; for when her cove maunds at any door, if any poultry be near, she feeds them with bread, and has a thread tied to a hook, baited. The chicken, swallowing this, is choked, and hidden under the cloak. Chickens, linen, clothing, or anything that is worth the catching, comes into her net.
*O Per Se O*

*Note*: 'when her cove maunds' – when her man begs (vagabond slang)

1 What does the vagabond woman carry?
2 What skills does she pretend to have?
3 How does she catch chickens?
4 What other things does she steal?

## Gypsies

Gypsies came to England in the first half of the sixteenth century. Many people disliked

**Figure 3** Gypsy telling Fortunes

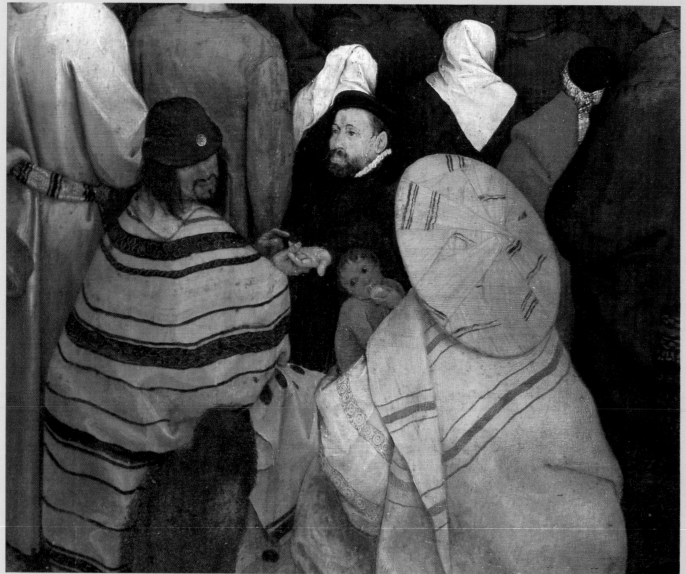

them. This was because they were foreigners. It was also because they wandered about the countryside, refusing to settle down and work. As a result, a law was made saying that gypsies should be deported. Any that were caught were taken to the coast. There, they were put on the next ship, no matter where it was going. This cruel law did rid the country of gypsies for a time, but they soon returned.

Thomas Dekker describes gypsies:

*Document Eight*
They are usually in an army about four score strong, but they never march together, but four five or six in a company. These vagbonds have their women with them and a number of little children; which young brood of beggars are sometimes carted, like so many geese alive to market, in pairs of baskets. But if they are old enough, they sit on the horse, seven or eight of them, and tied together. Like flocks of wild geese they will evermore fly one after another. Wherever the leaders go, they stick up small boughs in several places which serve as flags to wave on the rest.

The places where these land-pirates lodge in the night are the barns of farmers and husbandmen, who dare not deny them, for fear they should before morning have their thatched houses burning about their ears. These barns are their kitchens, their supping-parlours and their bedchambers; for there they cook, after a beastly fashion, whatever they have stolen. Sometimes they eat venison, and have greyhounds that kill it for them.
*Lantern and Candlelight*

1 How many are there in an 'army' of gypsies?
2 How large are the groups in which they travel?
3 How do they carry their children?
4 How do the leaders show which way they have gone?
5 Where do gypsies stay at night?
6 Why do the owners of such places allow this?
7 How do gypsies obtain their food?

Dekker also wrote:

*Document Nine*
Their dress is odd and fantastical, though full of rents. The men hang their bodies with bells and other toys, to entice the country people to flock about them and to wonder at their fooleries.

The simple country folk will come running to gaze upon them, while in the meantime, one creeps into their houses and steals whatever he can lay hold on. On holidays they spread themselves in small companies among the villages, and when people flock about them they then say they have skill in palmistry and can tell fortunes. Often they are right. For one of them will tell you that you shall shortly have some evil luck, and within half an hour you shall find your pocket picked or your purse cut. These are the Egyptian grasshoppers that eat up the fruits of the earth. To sweep these swarms out of this kingdom, there are no other means but the worst kinds of punishments.
*Lantern and Candlelight*

1 Why do gypsy men hang bells on their clothes?
2 What do the country folk do when gypsies come into a village?
3 How do gypsies take advantage of this?
4 What skill do gypsies claim they have?
5 According to Dekker, what should be done to gypsies?

Study this picture of gypsies:

**Figure 4**  Gypsies   Who are the people on the horse? What is the woman on the far right doing to the man?

# D  Vagabond Language

Vagabonds had a language of their own. Thomas Dekker explains why:

*Document One*
It was necessary that a people doing so many wicked things should make up a language which none but themselves should understand; and for that cause was this language which some call 'Pedlars' French' invented. Even if spies steal into their companies to discover them, they can freely speak one to another and yet avoid the danger. The language of 'canting' they study even from their infancy, that is, from the very first hour they call themselves 'kinchin coes', till they are grown into 'upright men'.
*Lantern and Candlelight*

1  Why do vagabonds have their own language?
2  What name does this language have?
3  When do vagabonds start to learn this language?
4  What is a 'kinchin coe', do you suppose?

Here are some words used by vagabonds:

| | |
|---|---|
| 'beak' – magistrate | 'lift' – rob a shop |
| 'booze' – drink | 'mort' – woman |
| 'chats' – gallows | 'nab' – head |
| 'couch a hogshead' – go to sleep | 'peck' – food |
| 'cove' – fellow, man | 'pigeon-holes' – stocks |
| 'draw' – pick a pocket | 'prancer' – horse |
| 'foist' – pickpocket | 'prig' – steal |
| 'glaziers' – eyes | 'stamps' – legs |
| 'greenmans' – fields | 'stow you!' – shut up! |
| 'ken' – house | 'walking mort' – vagabond woman |

Can you guess the meaning of 'boozing ken' and 'prigger of prancers'?

The word for 'thing' was 'cheat', and the vagabonds used it a lot. Here are some examples:

| | |
|---|---|
| 'belly cheat' – apron | 'smelling cheat' – garden |
| 'crashing cheats' – teeth | 'stamping cheats' – shoes |

See if you can guess these. The first are parts of the body, the second is a garment, and all the rest the farm animals:

hearing cheats; nab cheat; bleating cheat; cackling cheat; grunting cheat; lowing cheat; quacking cheat

After a time, honest people learnt the meanings of at least some of the vagabonds' words, and used them as slang. What slang words did you find that we still have today?

Here is a conversation between two vagabonds, with a translation:

*Document Two*
**Upright Man**  Bene lightmans to they quarroms! In what libken hast thou libbed in the darkmans, whether in a libbage or in the strummel?

(Good-morrow to thy body! In what house hast thou lain all night, whether in a bed or in the straw?)

**Rogue**  I couched a hogs head in a skipper this darkmans.

(I laid me down to sleep in a barn this night.)

**Upright Man**  I tour the strummel trine upon thy nab cheat and togman.

(I see the straw hang upon thy cap and coat.)

**Rogue**  I will lage it off with a gage of bene booze.

(I will wash it off with a quart of good drink.)
*O Per Se O*

Dekker tells us about vagabonds' nicknames:

*Document Three*
Olli Compoli is the name of one rogue, and these nicknames belong to others, namely Dimber Damber, Hurly Burly, General Nurse, the High Sheriff, the High Constable and suchlike. The woman also have nicknames, for some are called the White Ewe, the Lamb, etc.
*O Per Se O*

1  Make up some nicknames which would be suitable for vagabonds.

# E  Stories about Vagabonds

## 1  The Parson and the Robbers

One day two robbers came to an inn. As they sat drinking, they noticed a house, some distance away, that stood on its own. By pretending they were looking for a friend they tricked the land-lady into telling them all about the house. She said that a parson lived there, with just two servants, one of them an old woman, and the other a boy. The two men decided it would be easy to rob the parson, and that night they set off. Here is what happened:

**Figure 1**  The Vagabonds put a horselock on the parson's arm.

*Document One*
So they marched merrily towards this parson's house, viewed the same well and then hid in a wood. Said one of them to his fellow, 'Thou seest that this house is well walled about and that we cannot break in. Thou seest also that the windows have thick bars and there is no creeping in between. Therefore we must use some trick. I have a horse lock with me, and this I hope shall serve our turn.'

So when it was about twelve of the clock, they came near the house and lurked near the bedroom window. The dog of the house barked, and the priest waked out of his sleep. Then one of the rogues makes a pitiful noise, asking for Christ's sake some relief, that was both hungry and thirsty and was like to lie outdoors all night and starve for cold unless he were given some small piece of money.

'Well,' said this parson, 'away from my house, or lie in one of my out-houses until the morning. And hold! Here is a couple of pence for thee.'

The parson opens his window, and puts out his arm to give his alms. The rogue takes hold of his hand, and calls his fellow which was ready with his horse lock. He claps the same about the Priest's wrist, and the bars standing so close together that for his life he could not pluck in his arm again. They told him that unless he would at least give them three pounds, they would cut off his arm from his body. So this poor parson, in fear to lose his

hand, called up the old woman that lay in the loft over him, and told her to take all the money he had, which was four marks.

'Well,' they said, 'Master Parson, if you have no more, upon this condition we will take off the lock, that you will drink twelve pence worth of beer tomorrow at the ale-house, and thank the good wife for the help she gave us.'

He promised faithfully he would do so, so they took off the lock and went their way.
*A Caveat for Common Cursitors*, 1566, Thomas Harman

*Notes:*   'mark' – 13s-4d
'horse lock' – lock for locking a horse, much as you would a bicycle

1  Why was it difficult to break into the parson's house?
2  How did the robbers make the parson feel sorry for them?
3  Why did the parson put his hand out of the window?
4  What happened as soon as he did so?
5  How much money did the robbers demand?
6  What did they threaten to do to the parson, if he refused?
7  How much money did the parson give them?
8  What promise did the parson have to make?

## 2 John Maneringe and his Pass

Sometimes honest people were forced to travel without money, because they were very poor. That meant they seemed just like vagabonds. Obviously, they did not want to be whipped, so they went to a magistrate, or someone important, and asked for permission to make their journey. If he agreed it was essential, he gave them a pass. A traveller with a pass was not punished. Instead, at each place he called, he was given a small sum of money to help him on his way. A pass might be like this one, which was carried by a man calling himself John Maneringe:

*Document Two*

To all Justices of the Peace, Mayors, Constables: Know that I, Lord Scroop of Bolton, Lord Warden of the Middle March of England and Captain of Her Majesty's City and Castle of Carlisle; give to everyone whom this shall concern that this bearer, John Maneringe, lately arrived in Scotland, bringing proof from the lord warden of Scotland, the cause of his arrival in that country. These are to certify you that the said John and others of his company (through tempest and foul weather) were driven ashore upon the north part of Scotland. Where they were by the north-landmen robbed of their Ship and all therein. Wherein the said John lost his own share, the value of three score pounds, besides being grievously wounded in the thigh with a dart, and in the arm with an arrow. This letter is to request you to let him pass unto Wornyll in Cornwall to his family and to help him according to Her Majesty's most gracious laws. I do allow him four months to pass unto the town of Wornyll by reason of his hurt; not able to go far in a day.

Given under my seal at Carlisle this 25th of March 1596. *Thomas Scroope.*

**Westmorland.** Allowed to pass this county, behaving well and honestly. *James Bellingham.*

**Yorkshire.** By me allowed to pass. *Timothy Whittyngam.*

**Stafford.** Allowed to pass this County 20th April, behaving himself honestly. *Thomas Crasley.*

**Woster Shire.** Allowed to pass this County the 30th April. *Edward Horwell.*

**Gloster.** Allowed to pass this county. *Edward Wynter.*

1 What misfortune had John Maneringe suffered in Scotland?

2 Where was the pass issued? Where was Maneringe going?

3 How long was the journey? (Work this out from a map.)

4 How much time was Maneringe allowed to make his journey?

5 How many miles was that in a day, on average?

**Figure 1** John Maneringe's Pass It is still preserved in the British Museum.

James Bellingam
Timothy Whittyngam
Tho: Cresley
Allowed to pass this countye accordynge to the tenor within written
EdWynter

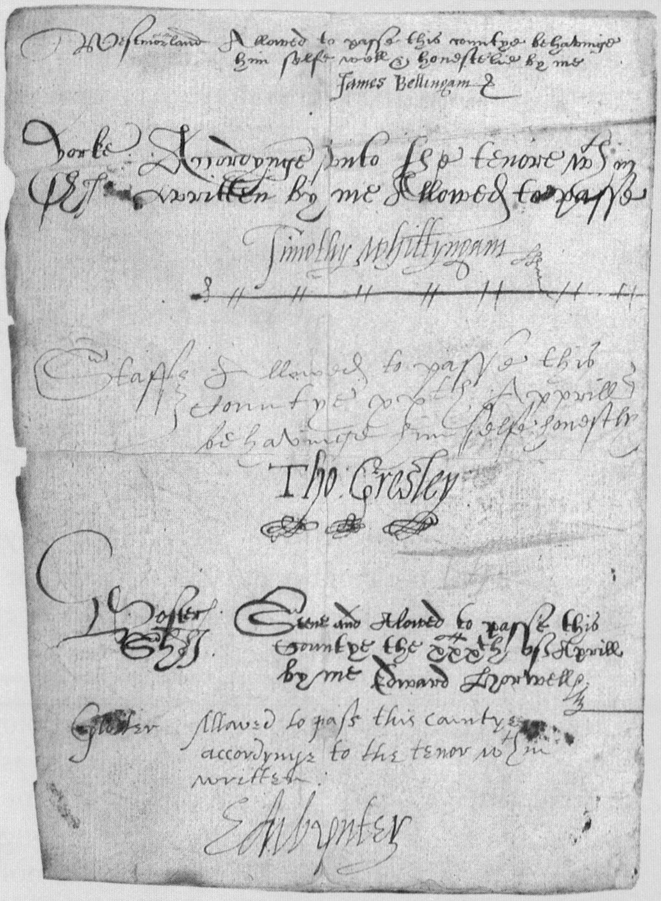

**Figure 2** Edward Hext questions John Maneringe

After Lord Scroop's signature are entries made by the magistrates who saw the pass. From them you can follow Maneringe's journey. Do this on a map showing the old counties. You will see that the last entry is for Gloucestershire, a long way from Maneringe's destination. The reason is that in Somerset, Maneringe fell into the hands of the magistrate, Edward Hext. Hext wrote to Elizabeth's chief minister, Lord Burghley:

*Document Three*
The bearer of this counterfeit pass is heir to much land after his father dies and his name is Limerick. His father is a gentleman and lives at Northleach in Gloucestershire. I kept him in prison for two months and questioned him often, and yet he still confirmed the truth of his pass with most horrible oaths. Accordingly I sent into Cornwall where he said his mother lived, and by that means discovering him, he confessed all. Your Lordship may see it is most hard to discover any vagabonds by questioning them, all being determined not to confess to anything. They feel sure that none will send two to three hundred miles to discover them for a whipping matter, which they regard as nothing.
*Letter to Lord Burghley*, 1596

1 What was Maneringe's real name?
2 Why was there no need for him to be a vagabond?
3 How did Hext prove the pass was forged?
4 How long did it take Hext to do this?
5 Why did he need so much time, do you suppose? (How were messages carried in those days?)
6 How would the police check a similar story today? How long would it take?

There were few magistrates like Edward Hext. As he says at the end of the extract, vagabonds knew they only had to lie, since hardly anyone would go to a lot of trouble to unmask them. Count the number of magistrates who just signed the pass and sent the man on his way.

You might like to know who forged the pass. It was the work of Ralph Bower, a schoolmaster living at Penreth in Cumberland. Forging passes for vagabonds was probably one of his side-lines.

# F  Measures against Vagabonds

From time to time Parliament passed laws against vagabonds. These laws all said much the same kind of thing. Here is an extract from one of them:

*Document One*
Every Rogue, Vagabond or Sturdy Beggar which shall be taken wandering in any part of this Realm shall be stripped naked from the middle upwards and publicly whipped until his or her body be bloody, and forthwith sent to the parish where he was born, there to put him or herself to labour as a true subject ought to do.

If any of the said Rogues appear to be dangerous, the Justices may banish them out of this Realm. And if any such Rogue so banished shall return again, he shall suffer death by hanging.
*Act for the Punishment of Rogues, Vagabonds and Sturdy Beggars*, 1597

1  How are vagabonds to be punished?
2  Where must they go after they have been punished?
3  What must they do when they arrive?
4  What vagabonds may be banished?
5  What will happen to them if they return?

Here are two orders that the Aldermen of London made about a beggar boy:

*Document Two*
**a.** Robert Shakysberie being but a boy and diseased with the palsy wherewith his body shaketh very sore, shall depart out of the city upon pain of whipping. (15 December, 1576.)
**b.** It is agreed that Robert Shakysberie who falsely pretends to have the disease of the palsy, and here loiters and continues begging contrary to the order of 15 December, shall according to the same order be whipped throughout the market places of the city at a cart's tail, and then be expelled out of the same city. (20 April, 1577)
*Reperties of the Court of Aldermen*

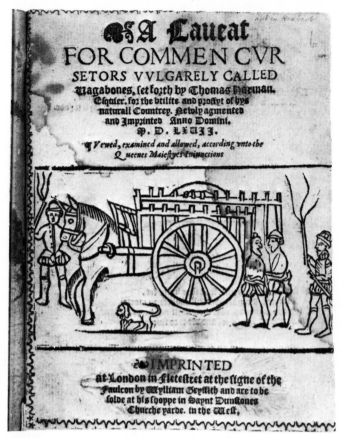

**Figure 1**  Vagabonds being Punished  How are these men being punished? Why have they been tied to a cart rather than a post, do you suppose?

1  What disease did Robert Shakysberie pretend to have?
2  What was he ordered to do?
3  What happened to him when he disobeyed?

From time to time, the government tried to make sure that the laws against vagabonds were being obeyed. Here is a letter which Elizabeth's ministers sent to the Aldermen of the City of London:

*Document Three*
You shall cause a thorough search and a good strong watch to begin on Sunday night about nine of the clock, and to continue the same until four of the clock in the afternoon of the next day, and in that search to arrest all vagabonds, rogues, or Egyptians, and all other idle vagrant persons. You are to imprison them in stocks and compel them by punishment to labour for their living.
*Privy Council to the London Aldermen*, 1569

1 How are the Aldermen to find the vagabonds in London?
2 What is to happen to the vagabonds when they are caught?

The government sent letters like the one you have just read, all over the country. The various authorities were supposed to write back and say what they had done. Here is a reply from Staffordshire:

*Document Four*
A Certificate made to Sir Walter Ashton, Sheriff of the County of Staffordshire. Touching the watches and searches for vagabonds and beggars, as followeth:

*Edward Greaves* with Agnes his wife. Being of the age of 43 years. Taken at Ashley and brought to Eccleshall where they were punished according to Law and afterwards sent by passport to Berkswell in the county of Warwickshire where they were born.

*Elizabeth Kingston*, widow, with one child. Taken by the watchmen of Wootton was brought to Eccleshall and punished and sent by passport to Newport where she was born.

*Fowlk Conway*. Taken by the Constables of Eccleshall, was brought before me, but having a passport was sent with the same to the next Constable homeward.

*Margaret Billington*. A poor woman, taken by the Constable of Staundon was brought to Eccleshall. But sent back again for that she had taken harvest work.
*Report of the Staffordshire Magistrates*, 1571

1 What happened to Edward Greaves, his wife, and Elizabeth Kingston?
2 What happened to Fowlk Conway? Why was he treated differently?
3 Why was Margaret Billington allowed to stay in Staundon?

Most of the time, little was done about vagabonds. Edward Hext gives some of the reasons for this:

*Document Five*
If they be caught by a simple man that has lost his goods, he is many times content to take his goods and let them slip. He will not then be bound to give evidence at the assizes, to his trouble and charge. Others are delivered to simple constables that sometimes wilfully, other times carelessly, allow them to escape. Others are brought before some Justice that either lacks the experience to question a cunning thief, or will not take the pains that ought to be taken in questioning him.
*Letter to Lord Burghley*

1 What is any ordinary person likely to do, if he catches a thief stealing his goods? Why?
2 What sometimes happens when a vagabond is handed over to a constable?
3 Why do many justices fail to deal properly with vagabonds?

Hext also wrote:

*Document Six*
There are three or four hundred idle people in every shire. Though they go by two and three in a company, yet many do meet either at a fair or market or in some alehouse once a week. And in a great hay house in a remote place there did meet weekly forty, sometimes sixty, where they did roast all kind of good meat. The inhabitants being much grieved by their stealing, made complaint and my Lord Chief Justice gave orders to the Tythingmen for their arrest. They made answer that the vagabonds were so strong that they dared not adventure of them.
*Letter to Lord Burghley*

*Note*: 'tythingman' – kind of village constable

1 What do the vagabonds in each county do once a week?
2 What was happening in the barn that Hext mentions?
3 What were the tythingmen ordered to do?
4 Why did they refuse?

There were vagabonds all through Elizabeth's reign, and for a long time afterwards. Indeed, we have people very like the sixteenth century vagabonds today. Who are they?

# 5 Crime and the Police

## A Introduction

We will ask a London lawyer about crime.

*'Is there much crime in England these days?'*

'A great deal, I am afraid. For one thing, there is a lot of violence. Almost everyone carries a sword or a dagger. Men drink, they quarrel, and when they begin to fight, they draw their weapons. At the end of the fray, someone lies bleeding on the floor, as often as not.'

*'Do many people make a living from crime?'*

'Yes, especially here in London. We have many criminals, some of them very clever. They are known as "cony-catchers." '

*'What is a cony?'*

'In thieves' slang it is someone who does not know how to look after his money. The simple countryman, in London for the first time, is the perfect cony. One such man went about the city proudly wearing a gold chain. As long as he kept it round his neck it was, of course, almost impossible to take it. But a gang of villains was determined to have it. Accordingly, one of them, dressed like a gentleman, went to him and said, "Sir, if you will be guided by me, you will hide your chain. If not, the cony-catchers are sure to steal it." The countryman thanked him warmly and put the chain out of sight in his pocket. "The cony-catchers shall not have it now," he said. Alas, picking a pocket is the easiest of things to these rogues. Shortly afterwards the poor countryman was jostled in a crowd, and when he came out of it, his chain was gone.'

*Note*: The proper meaning of 'cony' is 'rabbit'.

1 Give one reason why there are so many crimes of violence in Elizabethan England.

**Figure 1** Dagger Nearly all Elizabethan men carried weapons like this.

2 What name is given to the clever criminals in London?

3 Describe in your own words how the countryman was robbed of his chain. (The story is true.)

**Figure 2** Chains These are from the Cheapside Hoard.

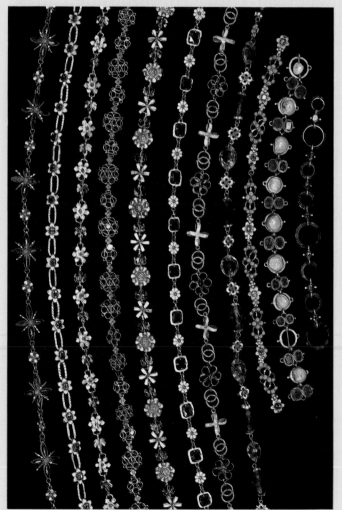

We will now talk with the constable of Winterborne Hinton, in Dorset. His name is Samuel Barton.

'*How did you become constable?*'

'I was chosen by the other villagers.'

'*That must have made you feel proud.*'

'Not at all. Being constable is a job we all have to take in turn, and no-one wants it. I certainly did not.'

'*Why is that?*'

'I am a farmer, and that means I am very busy much of the year. I cannot afford the time to do constable's work.'

'*Aren't you paid for it?*'

'No, of course not.'

'*How long must you be constable?*'

'For a full year, which is quite long enough. Then someone else will be chosen.'

'*Can we see your uniform, please?*'

'Uniform? There is no uniform! Everyone knows that I, Samuel Barton, am constable this year, so what use would a uniform be?'

'*What work do you do, as constable?*'

'I will tell you what I ought to do, which is not quite the same thing. My main task is to keep an eye on the village and see that everyone behaves themselves. The main problem is with the ale house. It is supposed to shut when there is a service at the church, there should be no drunkenness, and there should be no unlawful games, like cards and dice. Short of staying there the whole time, I can't see these laws are obeyed. Then sometimes there is a brawl. When one of those is reported, I don't hurry, I can promise you. With any luck, the fighting is over by the time I arrive.'

'*What do you do if anyone reports a crime, such as a highway robbery?*'

'I am supposed to raise the hue and cry. That means calling all the villagers to search for the criminal. You can imagine how unwilling they are to leave their work and hunt for a dangerous highwayman, just because some fool of a stranger has lost his purse.'

**Figure 3**  Lock-up, Bradford-on-Avon   This old chapel on a bridge was used for prisoners who were waiting to be sent to jail.

'*Are there constables like you all over England?*'

'Yes, but in the towns they have paid watchmen to help them'

'*There must be more law and order in the towns, then.*'

'Not at all. The watchmen are so badly paid that no-one will take the job if he can do anything else. Some of them are old, some of them are lame, and all of them are ignorant. They may arrest women and children they find begging, but if they run into any real trouble, most of them make off as fast as they can.'

1  How did Samuel Barton become constable?
2  Why did he not want the job?
3  How long will he be constable?
4  What is his main task?
5  What is his main problem?
6  What should he do, if a crime like highway robbery is reported?
7  Who helps the constables in the towns?
8  Why will no-one who is any good take this job?

# B Cutpurses, Pickpockets and the 'Black Art'

In the sixteenth century there were no banknotes, and, therefore, no wallets. People usually kept their money in purses hung from their belts. A thief might take the money by cutting open the purse, or, if he was really clever, by putting his hand in it. Cutpurses were called 'nips' and pickpockets were called 'foists.' Robert Greene tells us about them:

*Document One*
Their chief walks are St. Paul's, Westminster, plays, bear gardens, the Lord Mayor's Day, festivals, shooting matches or fairs. To be short, wheresoever there is a great crowd, there the nip and the foist have the best chance to show their juggling skills.

In St. Paul's their chiefest time is at divine service. There the nip or the foist stands soberly, with his eyes raised to Heaven, while his hand is on either the purse or the pocket, feeling every corner of it for coin. Then, when the service is done, and the people press away, he pushes into the crowd and there works his villainy.

A good foist must have three qualities that a good surgeon should have, and that is, an eagle's eye, a lady's hand and a lion's heart: an eagle's eye to spy out where the bung lies, and then a lion's heart not to fear what the end will be, and then a lady's hand to be little and nimble, the better and the more easy to dive into a pocket.
*The Second Part of Cony-Catching*, 1591

*Note:* 'bung' – thieves' slang for purse

1 What is the difference between the 'nip' and the 'foist'?
2 In what conditions do nips and foists like to work?
3 What do they do during the service at St. Paul's?
4 Why do they wait until the service is over before they steal, do you suppose?
5 According to Greene, what qualities must a foist have?

**Figure 1**  Purse   This was worn hanging from the belt.

Things were much more difficult for the nip and the foist if there was no crowd. Here is a story about two thieves who had this problem.

One day a nip and a lad he was training saw a man selling meal. The nip told his apprentice to show his skill by cutting the meal-man's purse. The apprentice refused. Apart from the odd customer there was no-one near the meal-man, besides which he kept handling his purse. Robert Greene tells us what happened next:

*Document Two*
'Dost thou count it impossible to have the meal-man's bung?' asked the nip. 'Go with me and do as I shall show thee. Begin a pretended quarrel and when I give thee a watchword, then throw flour in my face.'

As soon as they were come unto the meal-man, the old nip began to jest with the other about the miller's sack, and the other replied as knavishly. At last the elder called the younger a rogue.

'Rogue,' said he, 'darest thou dishonour me with such a base title?' And with that, taking a whole handful of meal out of the sack, he threw it full into the old nip's neck and ran away.

The old nip thus dusted with meal, begged the meal-man to wipe it out of his neck, and stooped down his head. The meal-man laughing to see him so whited, was willing to shake off the meal, and while he was busy about that, the nip cut his purse, politely thanked him and went away. The poor man suspected nothing till he sold a peck of meal and offered to change for money, and then found his purse bottomless. He began then to exclaim against such rogues, and called to mind how, in shaking the dust out of the man's neck, he shaked the money out of his purse.

*The Second Part of Cony-Catching*, 1591

1  What did the apprentice throw over the nip's neck?
2  What did the meal-man do to help the nip?
3  What was the nip able to do, as a result?
4  When did the meal-man find he had been robbed?

Robert Greene tells us about the 'black art.'

*Document Three*
The black art is picking locks, and to this busy trade, two persons are needed, the charm and the stand. The charm is he that does the deed, and the stand is he that watches. The charm has many keys and wrests, which they call picklocks, and they will undo the hardest lock, though never so well warded, even while a man may turn his back. Well may it be called the Black Art, for the Devil cannot do it better than they.

I once saw the experience of it myself, for, when I was in the Counter there came in a fellow famous in the black art. I made friends with him, to find out about his art. One day, being in my chamber, I showed him my desk, and asked him if he could pick that little lock that was so well warded, and too little, as I thought, for any of his gins.

THE
SECOND
and laſt part of Conny-catching.

*With new additions containing many merry tales of all lawes worth the reading, becauſe they are worthy to be remembred.*

Diſcourſing ſtrange cunning in Cooſnage, which if you reade without laughing, Ile giue you my cap for a Noble.

*Mallem non eſſe quam non prodeſſe patrie.*

R. G.

LONDON.
Printed by Iohn Wolfe for William Wright.
1592.

*Not in Ames's H. of Printing*

**Figure 2**  The Black Art   This is from the title page of Greene's book. It is difficult to understand why Greene has the 'charm' drawn as a rabbit.

'Why, sir,' says he, 'let me come to your desk and do but turn five times round, and you shall see my skill.' With that I did as he told me, and before I had turned five times, his hand was inside my desk. I wondered at it, and thought truly that the Devil was in his fingers.

*The Second Part of Cony-Catching*, 1591

*Notes:*  'well-warded' – having good wards. Wards are the levers in a lock, which are turned by the key.
'the Counter' – one of the prisons in London. As you can see from this extract, the prisoners there did much as they pleased.

1  What is the 'black art'?
2  Why does it have that name?
3  How long, roughly, did it take the 'charm' to pick Greene's lock?

49

# C  Cheating at Cards and Dice

A man called Gilbert Walker describes one of the many ways of cheating at dice. A cheater is explaining some of his tricks. It will help you to know that novem quinque was a game in which players threw two dice, hoping to score nine or five.

### Document One

'Lo, here,' says the cheater to the young man, 'a dice that seems good and square, yet is the forehead longer on the four and three. Such be called "barred four-threes" because the longer end will, of his own accord, fall downwards, and turn up six, five, two or one. The main use of them is at novem quinque. So long as a pair of barred four-threes be walking on the board, so long can ye cast neither 5 nor 9; for without four and three, ye know that ye can never score five or nine.'

'How do they bring the dice in and out?'

'By a jolly fine shift called "foisting": and it is nothing else but a trick to carry them easily in the hand as long as long as the foister wants.'

'I do not understand how a man might carry dice in one hand, and chop and change them so often, and the thing not be seen.'

'Such jugglers' tricks seem impossible to understand till ye know their secrets. And true it is, to foist finely and readily, and with the same hand to pass money to and fro, is a thing difficult to learn and asketh a bold spirit and long experience.'

*A Manifest Detection of the use of dice play*

1  What two numbers cannot be thrown with the false dice described here?
2  What scores cannot be made with two of these dice? Check for yourself to see that this is so.
3  When will a cheat want ordinary dice in play, do you suppose?
4  How does he change the false dice for ordinary dice and back again?

Gilbert Walker also describes cheating at cards:

**Figure 1**  Playing Cards

*Document Two*
They have such skill in sorting and shuffling of the cards that ye will always lose. Some prick their cards with pins: some pinch the cards with their nails; some turn up the corners: some mark them with fine spots of ink. Other helps I have heard of besides; as, to set the victim upon the bench with a great looking-glass behind him on the wall, in which the cheater might always see what cards were in his hand. Sometimes they work by signs made by some of the lookers-on. Wherefore methinks this was a fine invention. A player, after he had been caught by the cheaters grew very suspicious, and would not allow any of the spectators to see his cards. For this the cheaters devised a new shift. A woman would sit beside him and by the movement of her needle show the cheater what were the victim's cards.
*A Manifest Detection of the use of dice play*

1   What are card cheats very clever at doing?
2   How do they mark their cards?
3   How do they find out what cards their victims are holding?

One of the main problems cheats had was to persuade people to play with them. Robert Green describes how it might be done. Three men were needed. They were the 'setter', the 'verser' and the 'barnard.'

*Document Three*
As soon as they see a plain country fellow, well and cleanly dressed, 'There is a cony,' says one. At that word, out flies the setter, and overtaking the man, greets him thus: 'Sir, God save you, you are welcome to London! How are all our good friends in the country?' The countryman, puzzled at this greeting from a man he knows not, perhaps makes him this answer: 'Sir, all our friends in the country are well, but truly, I know you not.' 'Why, sir,' says the setter, 'I know you by your face, and have been in your company before. I pray you, let me ask your name and where you live.' The simple man straight tells him where he dwells, his name and who be his next neighbours and what gentlemen dwell about him. Then the setter says, 'Sir, hold me excused, for I took you for a friend of mine.'
*Notable Discovery of Cozenage*, 1591

*Note:*   'cony' – someone easy to cheat or rob

1   What does the setter pretend?
2   What does the cony tell him?

Robert Green goes on:

*Document Four*
Then away goes the setter and tells the verser the name of the man, the village he dwells in and what gentlemen are his near neighbours. With that, the verser meets the man at some turning, and greets him thus: 'What, Goodman Barton, how are all our friends? I have the wine for you. You are welcome to town.' The poor countryman, hearing himself named by a man he knows not, marvels, and answers that he knows him not and asks his pardon. 'Not me, Goodman Barton, have you forgot me? Why, I am such a man's kinsman, your neighbour. How is this or that gentleman, my friend? Good Lord, that you should have forgotten me!'
'Indeed, sir,' says the farmer, 'are you such a man's kinsman? I have clean forgot you, but I know the good gentleman your cousin well.'
   'And for his sake,' says the verser, 'we'll drink before we part.'
   So to the wine or ale they go. Then, before they part, they make him a cony and so cheat him at cards that they leave him as bare of money as an ape of tail.
*Notable Discovery of Cozenage*, 1591

The third member of the gang, the barnard, pretends to be a drunken idiot. He joins the group and suggests a game of cards. He looks so easy to cheat that the cony cannot resist playing with him. In fact, the barnard is neither drunk nor an idiot, so he cheats the cony quite easily.

1   What does the setter tell the verser?
2   How does the verser persuade the cony that he knows him?
3   What, probably, will the cony agree to do?
4   What happens to him as a result?

## D Hookers

The magistrate, Thomas Harman, describes hookers:

*Document One*
They carry with them a staff five or six feet long, in which, within one inch of the top is a little hole bored. In this hole they put an iron hook. With the same they will pluck unto them quickly anything that they may reach. The hook, in the day-time they hide, and is never taken out till they come to the place where they do their stealing. Such have I seen at my house, and have oft talked with them and have handled their staves, not then understanding to what use they served. They will either lean upon their staff to hide the hole when they talk to you, or hold their hand upon the hole.
*A Caveat for Common Cursitors*, 1566

*Note*: Anyone who carried a six foot staff today would soon be noticed. But in the sixteenth century, many poor travellers had them.

1 Why does a hooker have a hole in his staff?
2 What does he do with his hook in the day-time?
3 How does he hide the hole in his staff, when he talks to people?

Most hookers used their hooks to steal clothes spread to dry on hedges, or to take things through the open windows of rooms where there were no people. Here, though, is Harman's story of a hooker who was braver than most:

*Document Two*
A hooker came to a farmer's house in the dead of night. He opened the window of a low bedroom, and saw a bed in which lay three persons (a man and two big boys). This hooker with his staff plucked off their garments which lay upon them to keep them warm, with the coverlet and sheet, and left them asleep naked, saving their shirts. I verily suppose that when they were waked with cold, they thought that

**Figure 1**  Hooker at work

Robin Goodfellow had been with them that night.
*A Caveat for Common Cursitors*, 1566

*Note*: 'Robin Goodfellow' – mischievous fairy

1 What did this hooker steal?
2 What shows he was very clever?

Here is another story about hookers:

*Document Three*
A hooker and his warp came by a nobleman's house near London and saw the window of the porter's lodge open. Looking in, he spied fat snappings and bade his warp watch carefully, and took his hook and thrust it into the chamber. The porter lying in his bed, was awake and saw all, and so did the yeoman of the wine cellar who shared his room. The porter stole out of bed to see what could be done.

The first snapping the hooker picked up was a coat. As he was drawing it to the window, the porter gently lifted it off, and so the hooker drew his hook in vain. Meanwhile the yeoman of the wine cellar stole out of the bedchamber, and raised up two or three more, and went out to take them. But still the rogue did his work and picked up a gown, but when it came to the window, the porter lifted it off the hook so gently the hooker felt nothing. Then when he saw his hook would take no hold, he swore and grumbled and told the warp he had hold of two good snaps and missed them both, and that the fault was in the hook. To make it better, he then fell to sharping and hammering of the hook and in again he thrust it and picked up a pair of hose. But when he had drawn them to the window, the porter took them off again, which made the hooker almost mad, and he swore he thought a Devil was abroad, he had such bad luck.

'Nay,' says the yeoman of the cellar, 'there is three abroad, and we are come to fetch you and your hooks to Hell.'

So they took these base rogues and kept them in the porter's lodge. In the morning some gentlemen in the house sat for judges – in that they would not trouble their lord with such filthy caterpillars – and by them they were condemned to forty blows each with a bastinado.
*The Second Part of Cony-Catching*, Robert Greene, 1591

*Notes*: 'warp' – someone who keeps a look-out for a thief
'snapping' – thing worth stealing
'yeoman of the wine cellar' – servant who looks after the wine

1 What room did the hooker try to rob?
2 Why did the porter see what was happening?
3 What did the porter do when the hooker picked up his coat?
4 Who went to get help?
5 What did the porter do when the hooker picked up his gown?
6 What did the hooker blame for his failure?
7 What did the porter do when the hooker picked up a pair of hose?
8 Whom did the hooker blame this time?
9 Who arrested the hooker and his warp?
10 Who punished them? How? (Look up bastinado in a dictionary.)
11 What would happen, today, to anyone who punished a thief himself?

Here is a report from a modern newspaper:

*Document Four*

---

**CLOTHES HOOKED**
Thieves pulled £3,000 worth of dresses one by one through the letter box of a boutique in Southmead, Bristol, after dragging racks to the door with a 12-foot boat hook.
*Daily Telegraph*, 27 October 1984

---

1 Would it be correct to describe these modern thieves as 'hookers'?

# E  Dishonest Horse Dealers

You probably know that a dishonest car dealer can make a worn out vehicle seem as good as new for a few hours. Similarly, in the sixteenth century there were dishonest horse dealers who played all sorts of tricks with useless horses.

A common disease of horses was glanders. One of the symptoms is a running nose. Thomas Dekker tells us what a horse dealer might do to a horse with glanders:

*Document One*
In the very morning when he is to be sold, the horse dealer tickles his nose with a good quantity of sneezing powder, which is blown up into the nostrils to make it work better. Next, he pokes up and down two long feathers dipped in the juice of garlic, which he thrusts to the very top of his head, to make the poor beast discharge the filth from his nostrils. This being done, he mixes the juice of garlic, strong, biting mustard and strong ale together, and into both nostrils is poured a good quantity of this filthy broth. With a little sneezing more his nose will be cleaner than his master's and the filth stopped so that for eight or ten hours the jade will hold up his head with the proudest gelding that gallops scornfully by him.
*Lantern and Candlelight*, 1608

*Notes*:  'jade' – useless, worn-out horse
'gelding' – male horse

1  What things are put up the horse's nose?
2  What effect do they have on him? How long will it last?

Here is another of the dealers' tricks:

*Document Two*
If the jade be so old that several teeth are dropped out of his head, then there is a trick to prick his lips with a pin till they be so tender that he will allow no-one to look him in the mouth, which is one of the best ways to tell his age.
*Lantern and Candlelight*, 1608

**Figure 1**  Horse Market  There were many dishonest dealers at markets like this.

1 Why should anyone buying a horse want to look in his mouth?
2 How does the dealer stop this happening?
3 We still have an expression, 'Don't look a gift horse in the mouth.' What does it mean?

Dekker also wrote:

*Document Three*
Whenever a horse dealer has a lumpish, slow jade that goes more heavily than a cow when she trots, and that neither by a sharp bit nor a tickling spur can he put him out of his lazy and dogged pace, what does he do with him? He gives him lamb-pie. That is to say, every morning when he comes into the stable he takes a cudgel and attacks the poor horse with it on the sides and buttocks. He never stops till he hath made them so tender that the very shaking of a bough will make the horse run out of his wits. Having thus learnt this hard lesson by heart, he comes into Smithfield to repeat it. The rider no sooner leaps into the saddle, but the horse dealer giving the jade, that is half-scared out of his wits already, three or four good bangs, away flies Bucephalus as if young Alexander were upon his back. No ground can hold him; no bridle rein him in. He gallops away as if the Devil had hired him, and goes through thick and thin, as if crackers had hung at his heels.
*Lantern and Candlelight*, 1608

*Notes*: There was an important horse fair at Smithfield.
'Bucephalus' – the famous horse of Alexander the Great

1 What is the problem with the horse described here?
2 What is 'lamb-pie'?
3 How does 'lamb-pie' affect the horse?
4 What is the person buying the horse likely to think of him?
5 What would happen, today, to anyone caught treating horses in the way Dekker describes?

# F  Highway Robbery

A traveller describes how he was robbed:

*Document One*
Faith, I have had a foolish odd mischance that angers me. Coming over Shooter's Hill, there came a fellow to me like a sailor and asked me money: and while I stayed my horse to draw my purse, he takes advantage of a little bank and leaps up behind me, whips my purse away, and, with a sudden jerk, threw me at least three yards out of my saddle. I was never so robbed in all my life.
*Sir John Oldcastle*, Michael Drayton 1600

1 Why did the traveller stop?
2 How did the highwayman rob him?

Ned Browne, a highwayman, says what he did to escape capture:

*Document Two*
I had for myself artificial hair, and a beard so naturally made, that I could talk, dine and sup in it, and yet it should never be spied. I have robbed a man in the morning and come to the same inn and dined with him the same day. For my horse that he might not be known, I could ride him one part of the day like a goodly gelding with a large tail hanging to his fetlocks, and the other part of the day I could give him a cut, for I had an artificial tail so cleverly made, that the ostler when he groomed him could not notice it. As for my cloak, it was made with two outsides so that I could turn it how I wanted, for however I wore it, the right side seemed to be outward. By these methods I little cared for hues and cries, but disguising myself, would escape them all.
*The Black Book's Messenger*, Robert Greene, 1592

*Note*: 'hue and cry' – chase after a criminal

1 How did Browne disguise himself?
2 How did he disguise his horse?
3 How was his cloak made?
4 How do robbers try to escape without being detected, today?

# G  The Hue and Cry

As you saw in the introduction, one way of trying to catch criminals was by raising the 'hue and cry'. It was a very old system that had been used during the Middle Ages. William Harrison describes it:

*Document One*

For the better arrest of thieves and murderers there is an old law which says that if any man reports robbery or murder, the constable of the village where he comes and asks for help is to call out all the villagers, and to search woods, groves, and all suspected houses where the criminal may be: and not finding him there, he is to give warning to the constable in the next parish, and so on from parish to parish until the offender is found. Certainly that is a good law; however, I have known criminals to have escaped out of the stocks, being rescued by others for want of watch and guard. I have heard, too, that thieves have been let go because the villagers would neither take the trouble, nor pay the cost of taking them to prison, if it were far off; that when hue and cry have been made even to the faces of some constables, they have said, 'God restore your loss! I have other work to do at this time.'

*The Description of Britaine, 1578*

1  Whom should a constable call out, if someone reports a robbery or a murder?
2  Where should they search?
3  What should the constable do, if the criminal is not found?
4  Why do criminals, who have been captured, sometimes escape from the stocks?
5  What will villagers sometimes do, rather than take a thief to prison?
6  What have some constables said, when asked to raise the hue and cry?

Here is an account of a hue and cry from Leicester:

*Document Two*

This day Godfrey Cowper, one of the constables of the town of Leicester, did receive a bill of hue and cry – namely to search for one man that rode on a bay nag; he was wearing a white cloak, a white hat with a band of gold or copper with a star on his horse's face: item to search for one other man that rode on a black nag, a black cloak and a black hat, which had robbed certain men in the Forest of Sherwood. The said constable met with a young man riding on a bay nag, with a grey or whitish cloak, and the same coloured hat, and arrested him. His name, as he says, is George Harding. He says he serves Mr. Bevercotes of Bevercotes in Nottinghamshire, and his master is now at Glaston, and he came from there this morning with a sleeve of draw work which he delivered to Mr. Rudings. The Mayor then sent to Mr. Rudings to see if the story was true. He found it was, whereupon George Harding was set free. And the bill of hue and cry sent forward London way.

*Records of the Borough of Leicester, 1584*

*Notes:*  'bay' – reddish brown horse, with black mane and tail
'sleeve of draw work' – sleeve with fancy embroidery

1  Who was Godfrey Cowper?
2  How many men were described in the bill of hue and cry?
3  What had they done wrong?
4  Why did the constable arrest George Harding, do you suppose?
5  What did George Harding say he had brought to Leicester?
6  To whom did he deliver it?
7  How did the Mayor check George Harding's story?
8  What happened to George Harding, in the end?
9  What was done with the bill of hue and cry?
10  In your opinion, were the people of Leicester as slack as the villagers described by Harrison? (*Document One.*)

# H Curfew

One way to prevent crime was to stop people going out at night. Here is a by-law that was made at Leicester:

*Document One*
There have been within this town of Leicester riotous and evil persons who is not content all day to sit in Inns and ale-houses, to their great cost and loss of time, but likewise will do the same all night with walking in the streets. This is against the good laws of the realm and much trouble to the honest people that want to sleep. Other misfortunes come by such evil as, of late, the death of a man, which is to the great dishonour of Almighty God, the Queen's majesty and the great slander, hurt and trouble to this town.

Wherefore it is enacted that no person inhabiting the town of Leicester shall walk in any street of the said town after 9 of the clock at night and after the curfew bell do leave ringing. And if any such person be taken in the streets, for the first time he is to forfeit 12d., the second time 2s-0d., and the third time to suffer imprisonment at Mr. Mayor's will and pleasure.
*Records of the Borough of Leicester*, 1553

*Note*: The grammar in the first sentence is rather strange!

1 How have some of the people of Leicester been behaving badly?
2 How have they annoyed honest citizens?
3 What serious crime has there been?
4 What rule must the citizens of Leicester obey?
5 What are the penalties for breaking the rule?

Here is what happened one night at Devizes, in Wiltshire:

*Document Two*
This day Hugh Norris being taken in a search at midnight, lying in his garden, and being commanded by the constables to go and sleep in his house, refused to do so. He abused the officers in calling of them knaves, and refused to go

**Figure 1** The Bellman of London   The bellman is a watchman. What is he carrying? What does he have with him? As he walked, the man rang his bell, shouted the time, and warned people to lock their doors. He must have made it difficult for folk to sleep!

with them, so that they were forced to carry him. And the man being examined before Mr. Mayor and found guilty, was sent to the jail and there to sit with both feet in the stocks.
*Annals of Devizes*, 1584

1 What was Hugh Norris doing?
2 Why was he arrested?
3 How was he punished?
4 Do you think the police behaved reasonably on this occasion? Give reasons for your answer.
5 Do you think that imposing a curfew is a good way to prevent crime? Would it be a good idea to have a curfew today?

You can see how Shakespeare made fun of the police of his day if you read *Much Ado About Nothing*, Act Three, Scene Three.

# I The Arrest of Nicholas Jennings

Sometimes, people who were not police at all did police work. One day a magistrate called Thomas Harman went to London to see a man who was going to print a book he had written. From the window of his inn he saw a man begging. He was filthy, and his face was covered in blood. Harman thought he might be a 'counterfeit crank', that is, someone who pretended to be ill in order to make people have pity on him and give him money. Harman decided to find out and this is what happened:

*Document One*

I asked him where he was born, what his name was, how long he had had this disease, and how long he had been in London, and where.

'Sir', said he, 'I was born at Leicester. My name is Nicholas Jennings; and I have had this falling sickness eight years; and I have been these two years in London, and a year and a half in Bethlehem.'

'What is the name of the keeper of that house?' said I.

'His name is John Smith', he answered.

'Then,' said I, 'he must know you.'

'Not only he, but the whole house beside', said this crank.

I went into my room and commanded my servant to go to Bethlehem, and bring me word from the keeper whether any such man had been with him. My servant, returning to my lodging, did say that there was never any such man there. Then I sent for the printer of this book, told him of the crank, and asked that I might have some servant of his to watch him faithfully that day.

He sent two boys, that did as they were asked, and found the crank about St. Paul's. And when it began to be dark, he went to the waterside, and took a boat and was set over the water into St. George's Field. One of the boys took a boat and followed him, and the other went back to tell his master.

Soon, the master had taken a boat and crossed over. Now they still had sight of the

**Figure 1**  Nicholas Jennings in Two Disguises

crank, which crossed over the fields into Newington. The printer there stopped him and called for the constable. The constable would have laid him all night in the cage that stood in the street. 'Nay,' said the printer, 'I pray you have him into your house. For this is like to be a cold night and he has few clothes.'

The constable agreed. They had him in and made him wash, and stripped him stark naked.

Then the printer and the constable decided to search a barn for some rogues, a quarter of a mile from the house, and went about their business. The crank, spying all gone, asked the good wife that he might go out to the back of the house to make water. She bade him draw the latch of the door and go out, not thinking he would have gone away naked. But naked as ever he was born, he ran away.

*A Caveat for Common Cursitors*

*Notes:*  'Bethlehem' – hospital for the insane in London. Somtimes called Bedlam. London Bridge was the only bridge over the Thames, so people often crossed the river by boat.

1  What illness did Nicholas Jennings say he had?

2  How did Harman prove he was lying?

**3** Who watched Jennings all day?

**4** Who followed Jennings in the evening?

**5** Who arrested Jennings?

**6** Where was Jennings held?

**7** What was done to try to stop him escaping?

**8** How did Jennings escape?

**9** List the characters in this story, apart from Jennings, and say what each of them did. Which of the things done by folk, other than the constable, would be the job of the police today?

# J   Complaints about the Police

As you will see in the section on prisons, jailers made money from their prisoners. That meant they liked to have a lot of prisoners, much as a hotel owner likes to have a lot of guests.

A man called William Fennor spent some time in a London prison called the Counter. He wrote:

*Document One*
The more prisoners jailers have, the more is their gain. I have often heard them when my Lord Mayor's officers have brought in wrong-doers, whisper in their ears that they have had but a few prisoners that week. This is an encouragement to them to bring as many as they possibly can. Besides, they sometimes give a pint of wine to a beadle, that he might wake the watchmen if they should chance to sleep, and so might lose a night-walker.
*The Counter's Commonwealth*, 1617

*Notes*: 'Lord Mayor's officers' – beadles and watchmen, that is, the police. The beadles had charge of the watchmen.
'night-walker' – anyone breaking the curfew by being out late at night.

**1** What do jailers encourage the police to do?

**2** Why do jailers bribe beadles with wine?

While he was in the Counter, Fennor had this discussion with another prisoner:

*Document Two*
**Fennor:** I have often heard that the beadles and watchmen are in league with the jailers in the Counter, and that for every man they arrest, they receive a groat. Therefore they will, for the slightest fault, carry any man to prison. Also, I have seen many men come into prison that have been extremely hacked and maimed with their halberds. This should not happen, for though they have authority to arrest, they have none to kill or wound.

**Prisoner:** You say that the beadles and watchmen have for every man they arrest, a groat. Whether it be true or false I cannot say. If they have, it is fit that for so many nights as they stay up for the good of the city, they should have something allowed. And though there are many men hurt by the watch, the fault lies most of all in themselves and not in the watchmen. For when a company of gallants come from some tavern, high gone in wine and will not explain why they are out at such a late hour, but draw their swords and fall to hacking them, the watchmen are bound by law to arrest them and to defend themselves.
*The Counter's Commonwealth*, 1617

*Notes*: 'groat' – coin worth twopence
'halberd' – weapon like an axe with a very long handle

**1** According to Fennor:
   **a.** How much do the jailers give the police for everyone they arrest?
   **b.** How do the police often ill-treat prisoners?

**2** According to Fennor's fellow-prisoner:
   **a.** Why are the police entitled to money for making arrests?
   **b.** Who is to blame when prisoners are injured?

**3** With whom do you agree, Fennor, or his fellow-prisoner? If you cannot come to a decision say so, and explain why.

**4** What complaints are sometimes made against the police today? Compare these complaints with the ones made in the sixteenth century.

59

# 6 Punishments and Prisons

## A Introduction

We will ask a magistrate to tell us about punishments and prisons.

*'How do you punish criminals?'*

'Much depends on what they have done. If the watch finds a man wandering drunk in the streets, he will have to sit for a day in the stocks. If a baker sells loaves that are underweight, he will spend some hours in the pillory. There will be a paper over his head saying what he has done wrong. For any small offence a man may expect the stocks or the pillory.'

*'How do you punish more serious crimes?'*

'Often by whipping, or branding with a hot iron. This is how we serve rogues and vagabonds.'

*'Do you have capital punishment?'*

'All crimes known as felonies are punished by hanging.'

*'Please give us some examples.'*

'Murder is a felony, of course, and so are highway robbery and burglary. Stealing is a felony if the goods taken are worth more than a shilling. There are other crimes, too, which you might never imagine were felonies, like selling horses to the Scots.'

*'Why should a man be hanged for doing that?'*

'The Scots are England's enemies, and they could use the horses in time of war. A good horse will make a charger, and even an old jade will carry a soldier's baggage.'

*'What is the most serious crime of all?'*

'That is high treason, which is plotting to kill or overthrow the Queen.'

*'How is high treason punished?'*

'By hanging, drawing and quartering. First, the traitor is half-hanged, which means he is cut down before he is dead. Then he is dragged through the streets at a horse's tail. Finally, he is hacked in four, and his quarters put up in a public place so that all can see and take warning. Sometimes, though, the executioner will take pity on his victim and let him dangle on the gallows until he is quite dead. At least he will give him a hurdle to ride on for his drawing. That is better than being dragged, face downwards, through the streets. I should explain that noblemen are never hanged, drawn and quartered, nor are they even hanged. Their heads are cut off with the axe. It is a quick way to die.'

*'Do you use torture?'*

'Never. Though we hang many, we torture none.'

*'What about the instruments of torture in the Tower of London?'*

'They are not used for punishments, but to make dangerous criminals confess. If we know, for example, that a man has plotted to kill the Queen, he will go on the rack until he has confessed his guilt, and named his accomplices.'

*'You have not mentioned prisons. Don't you send criminals to prison?'*

'Very few. Most of the people in prison are not criminals. They are debtors. If a man owes you money, you can have him arrested and keep him in prison until he pays.'

*'How can a man pay his debts if he is in prison?'*

'You must remember that many debtors refuse to pay, simply to make life difficult for their creditors. A stay in prison usually makes them change their minds. If a man really cannot pay, his friends or his relations may take pity on him and pay his debts for him.'

*'How are people treated in prison?'*

'It depends on how much money they have. For example, in one of the London

**Figure 1**  Execution of a Nobleman by Beheading

prisons called the Counter there are three wards. They are the Master's Side, the Knights' Ward and the Hole. If a man has plenty of money he may go on the Master's Side, where he can live much as he would in an inn. He will order any food and drink he wants, he will sleep in a comfortable bed and he will receive visitors. If he has just a little money he will go into the Knights' Ward, which is not nearly as pleasant. If he has hardly any money, or none at all, he must go into the Hole. This is a wretched place indeed. Many lie there without beds. But even in the Hole, a man must find his own food.'

*'What happens to those who have no money?'*

'They depend on charity. Proctors go round the streets, begging for them. Without charity, they must die of hunger, which happens from time to time.'

1  What punishments are given for small crimes?
2  How are more serious crimes punished?
3  What name is given to crimes that are punished by hanging?
4  Give some examples of such crimes.
5  What is the most serious crime of all? How is it punished?
6  How might the executioner take pity on his victim?
7  How are noblemen executed?
8  When is torture used?
9  Who are most of the people in prison?
10  How can they gain their freedom?
11  Name the three wards in the Counter.
12  Who goes into the best of the wards?
13  What is it like there?
14  Who goes into the worst of the wards?
15  What is the only way that some of them can stay alive?

# B The Stocks, the Pillory and Riding the Skimmington

## The Stocks

Here is a picture of a man in the stocks:

**Figure 1** Minstrel in the Stocks

You can see that the stocks are divided into two. First, the top half was taken off, and the prisoner made to sit down with his ankle in the lower half. Then the top half of the stocks was put back and locked. The prisoner was held by one or both his feet.

1 Say why being in the stocks is not too bad for this prisoner.
2 Use your imagination and say how a day in the stocks would be unpleasant.
3 This man has a friend. What might happen if one of his enemies came along?

**Figure 2** Stocks at Falkland, Somerset. What was the lower of the two stones used for, do you suppose?

## The Pillory

Here are two people in the pillory. It is their punishment for pretending they could tell fortunes:

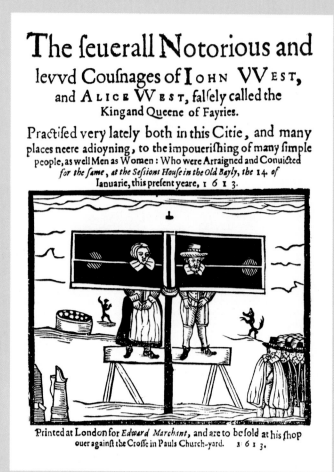

**Figure 3** Pillory

1 How is the pillory different from the stocks?
2 Which looks the more uncomfortable? Why?
3 Why are the prisoners made to stand on a stage do you think?
4 A crowd has gathered. Why is that, do you think? (If you heard someone was in the pillory, would you go and see? Why?)
5 If the crowd is angry with the prisoners, it may pelt them with all sorts of nasty things, even heavy stones. Can the prisoners protect themselves at all?
6 Imagine you are standing in the pillory. Describe your feelings.

**Figure 4**  Riding the Skimmington

Here is a notice that was pinned above two men who were put in the pillory in London in 1571:

*Document One*
These two persons have cheated with false cards and false play at the same, whereby they have robbed several persons of their money. And therefore it hath been thought good that they should stand here upon the pillory as an example to all such evil doers and cheats. And also so that all honest persons should see them and beware of them.

1  Why have the two men been put in the pillory?
2  What effect should this have on other cheats like them?
3  How will it help honest people?

## Riding the Skimmington

Figure 4 is a plasterwork frieze in the hall of Montacute House in Somerset. It is a bit like a strip cartoon. Study it and answer these questions:

1  On the left, there is a man in his house. He is supposed to be looking after the baby. What is he doing instead?
2  The man's wife comes in and catches him. What does she do to him? (The other man, standing outside the house, is probably the village constable.)
3  On the right, the guilty man is having his punishment. It is called 'riding the skimmington.' Describe what is happening. What do you imagine the people do, as the man goes round the village?

**Figure 5**  Finger Stocks (left)   These are unusual stocks. Lord Chief Justice Popham made each of his prisoners stand with one finger in these stocks, while he was being tried. The sketch shows why it was impossible for the prisoner to pull out his finger.

63

## C Punishment for Serious Crimes

An Essex clergyman called William Harrison describes some of the punishments for more serious crimes:

*Document One*
If a woman poison her husband, she is to be burned alive for petty treason; if a servant kill his master he also is to be executed for petty treason; he that poisons a man is to be boiled to death in water or lead, although his victim die not; in cases of murder all the accessories are to suffer pains of death by hanging. Perjury is punished by burning in the forehead with the letter P. Many crimes are punished by the cutting off of one or both ears from the head of the offender, as fray-making, petty robbers etc. Rogues are burned through the ears; carriers of sheep out of the land by loss of their hands.
*The Description of Britaine*, 1578

*Notes:* High treason, you will remember, was plotting to kill the sovereign. Petty, or small, treason was killing someone to whom you should be especially loyal. A wife should be loyal to her husband, and a servant to his master.

An accessory is anyone who helps a criminal commit a crime, or who shelters him afterwards.

A 'fray' is a riot or a brawl.

Rogues were wandering beggars.

1 What was the punishment for petty treason?
2 What was the punishment for poisoning someone?
3 What was the punishment for helping someone commit a murder?
4 What is perjury? How was it punished?
5 Name three other punishments which Harrison mentions.
6 How would you be punished for most serious crimes today?
7 One of the crimes mentioned by Harrison is not an offence today. Which is that?

Here is an entry from the notebook of the Town Clerk of Barnstaple, in Devon:

*Document Two*
At the assizes at Exeter this year, one Maynard had his ears cut off, his nostrils slit and burnt in the face with a hot iron with the letter F.
*Diary of Philip Wyot*, 1588

1 The **F** branded on Maynard's cheek stood for 'Felon'. The court must have taken pity on him, for it did not give him the most severe punishment for felony. What was that? (See *Introduction*.)
2 If Maynard was caught again, for another crime, it would be no use for him to pretend it was his first offence. Why not?

The most common way of executing criminals was hanging them. Probably, around 800 people were hanged in a year.

Here is a picture of a hanging:

**Figure 1**
A Hanging

A large crowd has gathered. The people in the windows probably paid the owners of the houses to let them go there.

1 There are armed men standing by. Why were they needed, do you think?
2 Why is the criminal blindfolded, do you think?
3 What does the man on the ladder seem to be doing? (It is difficult to see from such a small drawing, but, probably, he has a knife in his right hand.)

# D Punishments in Leicester

Leicester was a fairly typical English town, so it is interesting to know what punishments were used there. No-one who was living at the time has left us a proper description, but we can discover a great deal from certain old documents that have survived.

We have, for example, the chamberlains' account books. There were two chamberlains, and they were the men who looked after the town's money. Today, we would call them 'treasurers'.

Here is an extract from their accounts for 1554:

*Document One*

| | |
|---|---|
| Timber to make the gallows at the High Cross | 2–6 |
| Making the same | 2–0 |
| Setting the same in the ground | 6 |
| Two dozen points for the men that were harnessed at the execution of Kettell | 2 |
| Mr. Berredge for such things as was done about the execution of Kettell and setting up his head and quarters | 10–0 |
| Taking up the gallows at the High Cross | 2–0 |

*Records of the Borough of Leicester*

*Notes:* Being 'harnessed' meant putting on armour. 'Points' were laces. The town kept some suits of armour, but it looks as if they had been neglected, and needed new laces.

Berredge was the mayor.

The High Cross was the market cross in the very centre of the town.

We know nothing about Kettell, except what we can learn from these accounts.

1 From the payment made to Mr. Berredge, you can see that Kettell was cut into quarters. What does that show he had done? (See *Introduction*.)
2 Why were armed men needed at the execution, do you think?
3 Why was the High Cross chosen for Kettell's execution, do you think?

**Figure 2** Hanging, Drawing and Quartering

Here is an extract from the minute book of the town council:

*Document Two*
It is agreed that the old gallows shall be used again and made as big as they were before they were cut by order of Mr. William Morris when he was Mayor.
*Records of the Borough of Leicester*, 1582

1 What had Mr. William Morris done to the gallows when he was Mayor?
2 What does the town council order should be done with them now?

65

# E  The Counter Prison – The Knights' Ward

We are now going to visit the London prison that you read about in the *Introduction*. It is called the 'Counter.'

One day a man called William Fennor was walking along the street when a fat old merchant rushed out of a house. He was not looking where he was going and almost knocked Fennor over. Without thinking what he was doing, Fennor struck him with the flat of his sword. He was at once arrested and sent to the Counter, where he had to wait several weeks for his trial. While he was there he wrote a book about prison called *The Counter's Commonwealth*. You are going to read some extracts from the book.

When Fennor arrived at the prison he went into the Master's Side, but it was expensive and he ran short of money. The jailers then moved him to the Knights' Ward. He had already paid a lot of fees, or 'garnish', but this was what happened as soon as he arrived in the Knights' Ward:

*Document One*

I stepped into the Hall, where men were walking up and down as thick as merchants do on the Exchange. I greeted them and they bade me welcome when I was interrupted by a fellow I will thus describe to you. He was a tall, rawboned thing, and might very well have served instead of a maypole for all the hobnail wearers in the village to dance about. His face was wrinkled all over like an apple a year old. It was lean, and looked like a picture of Famine.

**Figure 1**  Newgate Prison   You can see that the prison was, as its name suggests, one of the gates of London.

**Figure 2**  Door from Newgate Prison displayed in the Museum of London.

His beard was so black that I thought he had a couple of black puddings round his chops. But he was as proud as a new made constable.

'Sir, are you a prisoner?' said he.

'Yes, sir,' said I.

'But,' said he, 'have you any money?'

'I have none,' said I, 'but my supplies will come in tomorrow.'

'Nay,' said he, 'I must not be put off. I must have a garnish of you of eighteen pence. I would not spare you if you were my father.'

I believed him, and therefore gave him fair words, telling him the next money I was blessed with, he should have.

At this answer he began to look as unpleasantly on me as a beggar on a whipping post; and he shouted three or four huge oaths, telling me that how I was treated would depend on how much money I had. This I found to be true, for at bedtime he brought me to a chamber near the privy that stinks worse than a jakes-farmer's clothes at twelve o'clock at night.

*Notes*: 'privy' – lavatory
'jakes-farmer' – man who emptied cess pits. Such people had to work at night because of the smell they made.

1 What room did Fennor go into?
2 Write a short description of the man who spoke with him.
3 What did he say Fennor must do?
4 Why did Fennor refuse?
5 What happened to Fennor in the evening, as a result?

When he woke the next morning, Fennor began to explore the Knights' Ward. This is what he found:

*Document Two*
I saw a cellar door standing open, so I stepped down. Being no sooner descended I saw a company of gentlemen, all prisoners, sitting at a table. They were making themselves exceedingly merry, being as brimful of beer as my heart was of sadness. Some had their pipes never out of their mouths, who puffed more smoke out of their noses than ever came out of Cold-harbour chimneys or any brewhouse in St. Katherine's. Some sang as merrily as if they had been as free as the mountain air. One asked me to join them and offered me half a can.

1 What were the men doing in the cellar?
2 How did they greet Fennor?

Fennor wrote this about his fellow prisoners:

*Document Three*
In Noah's ark there were all sorts of creatures; so in the Counter, there are all kinds of people. There lie your right worshipful poor knight, your distressed gentleman, your shopkeeper, your prating and juggling lawyers, – all there like so many beasts in the wilderness, desiring to prey one upon the other. I think there are as many sins looking through the bars of a prison as there are walking through the gates of a city. For though we are all prisoners, yet the reasons for it are different. Some are in for debt, some for crimes they have done. Others there are that are voluntary, who come in on purpose and who, if it pleased them, could keep themselves out.

*Note*: 'prating' – talkative

1 What different kinds of prisoner does Fennor mention?
2 Fennor gives three reasons for being in prison. What are they?

It will seem strange to you that anyone should be in prison of his own free will. For one thing, it is impossible to go to prison today, unless you have committed a serious crime. In Elizabethan times, though, all you needed was some help from a friend. You both pretended you owed him a lot of money, and he had you arrested for debt. When you wanted to come out of prison you simply pretended to pay your friend, and he ordered your release. Men might even do this to escape nagging wives. Highwaymen sometimes took refuge in prison, if they thought they were going to be captured. The police would hardly look for them in prison!

## F Jailers

Here is what Fennor said about jailers:

*Document One*
They are men that have only one idea, and that is to ask money. If a gentleman comes into prison that has his purse full of crowns, they will have no mercy over him. If he stays but one night, he must pay at least twelve shillings before he is discharged! He must pay twelve-pence for turning the key at the Master's Side door, two shillings to the chamberlain, twelve-pence for his garnish for wine, tenpence for his dinner whether he stays or no: and when he is discharged, it will cost him at least three shillings and sixpence more, besides sixpence for the porter.

*Note*: 'crown' – silver coin worth five shillings

1   According to Jennor, what is the only thing that interests jailers?
2   What fees must a man pay for just one night on the Master's Side?

Fennor also said about jailers:

*Document Two*
Drunken jailers poison poor prisoners with their stinking sour beer, which they sell as dear as if it were the best. We have scarce a pint of wine for a penny, and they will not let us send for it out of doors, where we may have far better. They break such bottles our friends send in for us. They serve us with drink that the worst jailer among them will scorn to taste: but when we are all locked up for the night, will send for better out of doors and will be drunk when many a poor soul is so dry that they are ready to choke.

1   What complaints does Fennor make about the drink served in prison?
2   What do the jailers do with bottles of wine that friends send to prisoners? Why do they do that, do you suppose?
3   What do jailers do when the prisoners are locked up for the night?

**Figure 1**   Meal Time in the Counter

# G  The Hole

Fennor describes the Hole:

**Figure 2**  Giving Alms to Prisoners

*Document One*

He that would see the strange miracles of God, let him take some long voyage to sea, and he that would see the miseries of man, let him come into this place, the Hole. It stinks many men to death, and is to all that live in it as the dog-days are to the world, a cause of diseases. Jerusalem when it was sacked had no more disasters than this place, for as there was famine in Jerusalem, so in this place there are many men that die from want of food. In Jerusalem there was sickness, so in this place, wherever a man looks, some poor soul lies groaning under the sorrow of some dangerous disease; the child weeping over his dying father, the mother over her sick child; one friend over another. So if a man comes here, he at first will think himself in some churchyard that has been filled with some great plague, for they lie together like so many graves.

*Notes*:  Fennor mentions Jerusalem because its inhabitants suffered dreadful hardships when it was besieged by the Romans in 70 AD.
'dog-days' – the hottest days of the year. If there was plague it was usually at its worst during the summer. People thought the heat caused the disease.

1  How do the people in the Hole suffer?
2  What does the Hole look like to anyone seeing it for the first time? (See the last sentence.)
3  What people are there in the Hole that would not be allowed inside a prison today?

Fennor also said:

*Document Two*

The Hole is like a city. Instead of a Lord Mayor and Aldermen, we have a Master Steward and twelve old prisoners that help him. All are elected by the prisoners. And here, as in a city, is a constable, chosen by the Master Steward. And lastly as in a city there are all kinds of trades. For here you shall see a cobbler mending old shoes, and singing as merrily as if he were in a shop outside. Not far from him you shall see a tailor sitting cross-legged like a witch on her cushion. In another place you may behold a saddler, wondering how to mend the old woman's crupper that is almost burst in pieces. You may have a physician here that for a pottle of sack will give you as good a medicine as any doctor will for five pounds and purge you thoroughly. If you wish to appear before a judge, you shall have a lawyer that will take all your money. Here is your bad-tempered cook, that will prepare our food, when we can get any, as well as any greasy scullion in Fleet Lane or Pie Corner. And twenty more than these there are which I could tell you.

*Notes*:  'old prisoner' – someone who has been in prison for a long time
'to purge' – to give someone a strong laxative. Elizabethans thought this was a cure for many illnesses.
'pottle' – half a gallon (about two litres)
'sack' – sherry

1  Who rules over the prisoners in the Hole?
2  How are they chosen?
3  What different jobs do people do in the Hole?
4  Were they glad to work, do you suppose? Give reasons for your answer.

# H  Stories about the Counter

Here is a story William Fennor told:

*Document One*

A poor man, having been two or three winters in the Hole, asked one of the keepers to go out with him, telling him he hoped to come to an agreement with his creditors. He was going to a friend to receive enough money to pay his debts. And if he would be good enough to go out with him, he would pay him. The keeper, who was as good at taking money as any leaking boat in taking water, went out with him. The best part of the day they spent walking up and down the City from friend to friend, yet they could not get as much as sixpence from any. When he saw there was no money to be had, the keeper would not stay a minute longer.

'Nay, faith,' said the prisoner, 'seeing you have been so good to stay out with me so long, let me go into a barber's shop and stay while I have my hair cut, which I have not had done this twelvemonth. And to reward you for your trouble, I will pay for you to have a shave.' The keeper, thinking to save a penny, went with him into the next barber's shop. The barber bids them welcome and falls first about the prisoner's ears, who, being finished, went to the window. The keeper took his place in the chair and started talking with the barber about what news he heard in the City. But they had not talked long when Cutbeard asked him to close his eyes, for fear the soap suds should come into them. The keeper did so. The prisoner then slipped out of doors, went quite away, and was never heard of again. The keeper, surprised he could not hear his prisoner talking, opened his eyes to see whether the prisoner were in the shop or no. He no sooner missed him, but up he jumps, and runs out of doors, knocking over the barber that came with his razor to shave him. He ran into the street with the barber's cloth around his shoulders, with his chops all white with the soap suds so that he looked like a boar that foamed at the mouth. Like this he runs madding up and down the street asking for his prisoner, while every man, woman and child gave him way, thinking he had just broken out

**Figure 1**   The Gaoler chases the Prisoner

**Figure 2** Cloak, Hat and Gloves  It was an expensive cloak, like the one shown here, that the chamberlain took from the prisoner.

of Bedlam. The barber followed him, laid hold on him, and got his cloth and his money of him, before he would let him go.

And so the keeper was forced to go back to the Counter without his prisoner. When the other jailers heard the story, they laughed him to shame. Moreover, he had to pay the prisoner's debts.

*Notes:*   It was quite normal for prisoners to pay jailers to take them out for a day.
'Bedlam' – a hospital for the insane in London. Its correct name was Bethlehem.

**1**   Pretend you are the prisoner. Tell your friends how you escaped from the Counter.
**2**   Now pretend you are the jailer. What did you say when you returned to the Counter without your prisoner? (Tell as good a story as you can, but without any lies.)

Here is another of William Fennor's stories:

*Document Two*
A gentleman came into the Master's Side, and being ordered to pay his fees, told them there were none due, and none would he pay. The chamberlain took this very badly and thought he would one way or other be even with him. Early next morning, before the gentleman was up, he came into his chamber and took his cloak. When the gentleman awoke, he found his cloak missing, and heard the chamberlain had got it for his fees. Upon this, he went and demanded his cloak, but the chamberlain refused to deliver it, unless he would pay his fees. 'For,' said he, 'you have met with no fools.'

'No, faith,' said the gentleman, 'I rather think I am come among a crew of cunning knaves.' And at once he sent a letter to a Justice demanding a warrant for the arrest of the chamberlain, charging him with felony. When he was served with this warrant, the chamberlain would have given the gentleman his cloak again, but he refused. He was at last persuaded to take it on condition the chamberlain forgave him all the fees demanded of him. But the gentleman afterwards died here in misery, plagued by the keepers. They thrust him into the Hole, being winter, where, lying without a bed, he caught such a bad cold in his legs, it was not long before he died.

*Notes:*   'chamberlain' – treasurer
'felony' – crime punished by death. Stealing anything as valuable as a cloak was a felony.

**1**   Why did the chamberlain take the prisoner's cloak?
**2**   What action did the prisoner take against the chamberlain?
**3**   Why did that worry the chamberlain, do you suppose?
**4**   What agreement did the prisoner make with the chamberlain?
**5**   How did the jailers take their revenge on the prisoner?

# 7   Witchcraft

## A   Introduction

From the 1560's to the end of the seventeenth century, many people had a great fear of witches. It is hard to undersand why. This fear was greatest in East Anglia, especially in the county of Essex. Again, it is hard to understand why.

We will go back to 1588 and ask an Essex judge to tell us about witches. His name is Lord Darcy.

*'Why do people hate witches so much?'*

'Because they are the friends of the Devil. They do his evil work, here on earth. I have my own reason for hating witches. They bewitched my father to death.'

*'What are you doing to stop them?'*

'In 1563, Parliament made a new law against witchcraft. Anyone practicing the evil art is to go to prison for a year. Anyone bewitching someone to death, is to be executed by hanging. It is now up to magistrates and judges like me to find and punish all the witches we can.'

*'Have you found any?'*

'We have found them in large numbers. There are many in Essex, more than in any other county.'

*'Why should that be?'*

'It is hard to explain.'

*'Perhaps the people of Essex are more superstitious than those in the rest of England.'*

'The people of Essex are very religious. That means they are well aware of the Devil and his works. Folk in the more backward parts of England are less on their guard.'

*'What makes you so sure there are such people as witches?'*

'In the first place, God has told us so. You have only to read your Bible. Is it not written in the Book of Samuel that Saul consulted the witch of En-dor?

Secondly, there are laws against witchcraft, not only in this country, but all over Europe. Governments would not make laws against a crime that did not exist.

Thirdly, we have the evidence of those who have been bewitched. There are a great many. They could not all be mistaken.

Finally, we have the confessions of witches themselves. Some have even admitted their crime on the gallows, when their confession could do them no good at all.'

*'Have witches much power?'*

'All the power of the Devil is theirs to command. They can do great things.'

*'Is not England at war with Spain, and expecting an invasion?'*

'That is so.'

*'Then why not ask a witch to destroy the Spanish fleet and army?'*

'To do so, our Queen would have to sell her soul to the Devil. This she could never do. She is a true Christian.'

*'Are the Spaniards true Christians?'*

'Of course not. They are papists.'

*'Then why don't they use witchcraft against England?'*

'I have answered enough of your questions and have no time for any more. You must forgive me. I have work to do.'

*Notes:*   Lord Darcy was a real man. He was the judge at a famous witch trial. This was the trial of thirteen women of St. Osyth, Essex, in 1582. You will read about it later.

'Witch of En-dor' – see *Samuel*, Book One, Chapter 28.

'papist' – follower of the Pope. It is an impolite word for Roman Catholic.

**Figure 1**  People Worshipping the Devil

1  When was there a great fear of witches?
2  Where in England was this fear strongest?
3  Why did people hate witches?
4  When did Parliament make a law against witchcraft? What were the punishments for  **a.** practicing witchcraft
   **b.** bewitching people to death?
5  According to Lord Darcy, why have so many witches been found in Essex?
6  Lord Darcy gives four reasons for believing in witchcraft. Explain what they are, in your own words.
7  According to Lord Darcy:
   **a.**  Why are witches powerful?
   **b.**  Why does the English government not use witchcraft against the Spaniards?
8  What question is Lord Darcy unable, or unwilling, to answer?
9  Think of some questions you would like to put to Lord Darcy yourself.

## B  Activities of Witches

As you saw in the Introduction, Parliament passed a law against witchcraft in 1563. The first trial for witchcraft took place at Chelmsford, in Essex, in 1565. Three women were accused, Elizabeth Francis, Agnes Waterhouse, and her daughter Joan. They all lived at the little village of Hatfield Peverel.

Here is part of a confession Elizabeth Francis made at the trial:

*Document One*
I learnt this art of witchcraft at the age of 12 years from my grandmother. She told me to renounce God and His word and to give of my blood to Satan, which she gave me in the shape of a white spotted cat. She taught me to feed the said cat with bread and milk, and to call it by the name of Satan, and to keep it in a basket. When I first had the cat Satan, I asked it to make me rich and to have goods. He promised me I should, asking me what I would have (for the cat spoke to me in a strange, hollow voice). I said, sheep, and this cat at once brought sheep into my pasture to the number of 18, black and white. They stayed with me for a time, but in the end did all vanish away, I know not how.

   I then desired a husband, namely this Francis whom I now have, and the cat did promise I should. We were married and had a child, but we did not live so quietly as I desired. Whereupon, I willed Satan to kill my child, being about the age of half a year, and it did so. When I still found not quietness, I asked it to lay a lameness in the leg of Francis, my husband. It did it in this manner. It came in a morning to Francis's shoe, lying in it like a toad. Putting on his shoe, he touched it with his foot, and he was forthwith taken with a lameness that will not heal.
*The Examination and Confession of Certain Witches at Chelmsford*, John Philip, 1566

*Note*:  A witch's animal, such as the cat Satan, was called a 'familiar'. As you can see from the picture on page 77, familiars could come in all sorts of shapes.

According to Elizabeth Francis:

1 Who taught her witchcraft? What age was she then?
2 What was she told to do with her familiar?
3 What animals did she ask for?
4 What happened to them, after a time?
5 Who was the husband the cat found for her?
6 What did she ask the cat to do to her baby?
7 What did she ask the cat to do to her husband?

Today, of course, any doctor would realise that Elizabeth Francis was mentally disturbed and would send her for treatment.

Here is part of the confession of Agnes Waterhouse. It seems that Elizabeth Francis gave her the cat Satan, after a number of years:

*Document Two*
When I had received the cat, to try what he could do, I willed him to kill a pig of my own, which he did. I gave him for his labour a chicken, and a drop of my blood. And this I gave him at all times, when he did anything for me, by pricking my hand or face and putting the blood to his mouth, which he sucked. The spots of the pricks are yet to be seen on my skin.

Another time, being offended with one Father Kersey, I took my cat Satan in my lap and willed him to kill three of this Father Kersey's pigs, which he did. I rewarded him as before with a chicken and a drop of my blood, which chicken he did eat up clean, and I could find neither bones nor feathers.

Also, falling out with one, Widow Gooday, I willed Satan to drown her cow, and he did so, and I rewarded him as before.

Also, falling out with one other of my neighbours, I killed her geese in the same manner.

Falling out with another neighbour and his wife, I willed Satan to kill him with the bloody flux, whereof he died. Likewise, because I lived unquietly with my husband, I caused Satan to kill him, and he did so about nine years past, since which time I have lived a widow.

I first turned this cat into a toad by these means. I kept the cat a great while in wool, in a pot, but I became so poor I needed the wool. I prayed in the name of the Father, and of the Son, and of the Holy Ghost that the cat would turn into a toad. Forthwith it was turned into a toad, and I kept it in the pot without wool.
*The Examination and Confession of Certain Witches at Chelmsford*, John Philip, 1566

*Note:* 'bloody flux' – dysentery

According to Agnes Waterhouse:

1 How did she first test the cat's powers?
2 How did she reward him?
3 How did she take revenge on Father Kersey and Widow Gooday?
4 How did she take revenge on other neighbours?
5 What did she do to her husband?
6 Why did she change the cat into a toad? Does anything strike you as odd about this story? (Apart from the fact that it is impossible to change a cat into a toad.)

Elizabeth Francis was sent to prison for a year. Agnes Waterhouse was hanged. She was the first person to be executed for witchcraft in England. Joan Waterhouse, who gave evidence against her mother, was found not guilty.

# C  Evidence against Witches

No-one can be punished for a crime, unless there is enough evidence to prove they are guilty. In this section you will see the kind of evidence that was used against witches.

As you already know, Agnes Waterhouse was said to have let her familiar, Satan, suck blood from her. This is how her trial ended:

*Document One*
Then said the Queen's Attorney, 'Agnes Waterhouse, when did thy Cat suck of they blood?' 'Never,' said she.

**Figure 1** Witch and a Horde of Demons

'No?' said he. 'Let me see.'

Then the gaoler lifted up her kercher on her head, and there were several spots on her face and one on her nose. Then said the Queen's Attorney, 'By my faith Agnes, when did he suck of thy blood last?'

'By my faith,' said she, 'not this fortnight.' And so the jury went together for that matter. *The Examination and Confession of Certain Witches at Chelmsford*, John Philip, 1566

1 What was there on Agnes Waterhouse's face and nose?
2 What was this supposed to prove?

Spots that made the skin look as if it had been sucked were called 'witch marks'. Anyone accused of witchcraft was searched for these marks. If they had them, they were almost certain to be found guilty.

Study Figure 1 and answer these questions:

1 How has the witch made the demons appear, do you suppose?
2 Do any of the demons remind you of animals that you know?

In 1582, thirteen women from the village of St. Osyth, in Essex, were tried for witchcraft. One of them was called Ciceley Celles. Document Two is some of the evidence that

75

was given against her:

*Document Two*
Then Thomas Death accused Ciceley Celles of bewitching George Battell's wife and his own daughter Mary. And Alice Baxter was pricked to the heart by a white imp, like a cat, which then vanished into the bushes close by. She was badly hurt, and could neither walk, nor stand, nor speak. All of which Ciceley Celles denied. But her denial did her no good, for she had witch marks, so was condemned.
*A Record of the St. Osyth Witch Trial*, Anon., 1582

**1** According to Thomas Death:
  **a.** How many people did Ciceley Celles bewitch?
  **b.** What happened to Alice Baxter?
**2** What other evidence was there against Ciceley Celles?

The thing to note about Thomas Death, is that he told the court what other people had told him. This is called 'hearsay evidence'. Today, it is not accepted. Why is that, do you think?

Here is some more evidence from the same trial. A woman called Annis Letherdall gave it against her neighbour, Ursula Kemp:

*Document Three*
Ursula and I had a little matter of business between us, but I did not keep my side of the bargain, knowing Ursula to be a naughty beast. So Ursula, in revenge, bewitched my child, and so badly that Mother Ratcliffe, a cunning woman, could do it little good. And as proof that it was Ursula who had so hurt the babe, the little creature of one year old, when I carried it past her house, cried, 'Wo, wo,' and pointed with its finger to the window.
*A Record of the St. Osyth Witch Trial*, Anon., 1582

*Note*: 'cunning woman' – 'white witch'. White witches claimed they could undo the harm caused by bad witches.

**1** Why was Annis Letherdall sure that Ursula had bewitched her child?
**2** Would you believe such evidence?

**Figure 2** A Witch Being Lowered into Water   This was to test whether the woman was a witch. If she sank, she was innocent. If she floated, she was guilty.

Here is some more evidence against Ursula Kemp. It was given by her own son Thomas, a little boy of eight:

*Document Four*
My mother had four imps at home – Tyffin, like a white lamb; Tilly, a little grey cat; Piggin, a black toad; and Jack, a black cat. And she fed them at times with milk and bread, and at times they sucked blood from her body. Also, my mother bewitched Johnson and his wife to death. She has given the imps to Godmother Newman, who put them into an earthen pot which she hid under her apron, and so carried them away.
*A Record of the St. Osyth Witch Trial*, Anon., 1582

According to Thomas Kemp:
**1** How many imps did his mother have?
**2** How did she feed them?
**3** What did she do to Johnson and his wife?
**4** What happened to the imps, in the end?
**5** Have you ever heard small children telling strange stories? If so, did you believe them?

Here is another extract from the report of Ursula Kemp's trial:

### Document Five

At first she would confess nothing, but upon the good Lord Darcy promising her that if she would confess the truth she should have favour, she confessed as follows. Bursting out with weeping and falling on her knees she said, 'Yes, I had the four imps my son has told of. Two of them, Tilly and Jack, were "hees", whose office was to kill unto death. Two, Tiffin and Piggin, were "shes", who punished with lameness and bodily harm only, and destroyed goods and cattle. I confess that I killed all the folk charged against me; my brother's wife, and Grace Thurlow's child making it to fall out of its cradle and break its neck, and I bewitched the little babe of Annis Letherdall.

But Mother Bennet also has two imps, the one a black dog called Suckin, the other, red like a lion, called Lyerd. And Hunt's wife has a spirit, too. One evening I peeped in at her window and saw it look out from a pot, and it had a brown nose, like a ferret.'

Putting herself on the country, she was nonetheless found guilty to be a witch and executed.

*A Record of the St. Osyth Witch Trial*, Anon., 1582

Notes:    Lord Darcy was the judge.
'putting herself on the country' – turning Queen's evidence or, as some would say, 'grassing.'

1   How did Lord Darcy persuade Ursula Kemp to confess?
2   Why did Ursula Kemp accuse the two other women, do you think?
3   Did Lord Darcy keep his promise?

This is what happened to Elizabeth Bennet. She was the woman who, according to Ursula Kemp, had the two imps Suckin and Lyerd. A man called William Byett said she had bewitched his wife:

### Document Six

The said Elizabeth Bennet was at first silent and would confess to nothing beyond that she

**Figure 3**   A Witch and Her Familiars

certainly had a pot, but no wool therein, and no imps to lay on it.

Then did the good Lord Darcy say to her, 'There is a man of great cunning and knowledge come over unto our Queen, which hath told her what witches be in England. I and other of her justices have received orders to arrest all we can find. They which do confess the truth of their doings, shall have much favour; the others, they shall be burnt and hanged.'

And hearing these words, she fell upon her knees, shedding tears, and confessed as follows: 'William Byett and I dwelt together as neighbours should, well and easily. But lately we have fallen out, because he called me "old witch" and did curse me and my cattle. So I

77

replied, saying, "Stop it Byett, for it will light upon thyself." And Byett's beast died forthwith. Then Byett's wife beat my pigs and made them sick. And once she ran a pitchfork through the side of one so that it was dead.

Two years ago there came to me two spirits, one called Suckin, being black like a dog, the other called Lyerd, being red like a lion. Once, Suckin tried to push me into the oven, whereby I burnt my arm. Another time, Suckin and Lyerd sat beside me when I was milking. The cow snorted, and ran away, spilling the milk. Upon praying to the Father, the Son and the Holy Ghost, they departed. Afterwards, I sent Lyerd to kill William Byett's beasts. But, instead, he plagued Byett's wife to death.' Elizabeth Bennet was thereafter condemned and sent to the gallows with Ursula Kemp.
*A Record of the St. Osyth Witch Trial*, Anon., 1582

1  What did Elizabeth Bennet refuse to admit, at first?
2  According to Lord Darcy:
   a.  Who has been to see the Queen, and what has he told her?
   b.  What have he (Lord Darcy) and the other justices been told to do?
   c.  What will happen to witches who confess?
   d.  What will happen to those who refuse?
3  According to Elizabeth Bennet:
   a.  What had William Byett been calling her?
   b.  What did Mrs. Byett do to her pigs?
   c.  What two spirits came to her?
   d.  What did they do to hurt and annoy her?
   e.  What did she tell one of the spirits to do?
   f.  What did he do instead?
4  Did Lord Darcy keep his promise to Elizabeth Bennet?

As you have seen, Ursula King and Elizabeth Bennet were persuaded to confess by false promises from Lord Darcy. Other women confessed for no obvious reason at all.

**Figure 4** Witches' Sabbath

Possibly, they really did think they were witches. Many of them were lonely old women, and it is more than likely that they were senile. That means their minds were no longer working properly, because of their old age.

# D A Sceptic: Reginald Scot

A sceptic is someone who will not believe anything until he has definite proof that it is right. One such man was Reginald Scot. While almost everyone in England was delighted at the execution of the St. Osyth witches, Scot thought the trial was both wicked and absurd. He wanted other people to know how he felt, so he wrote a book called *The Discoverie of Witchcraft*. Here is an extract from it:

*Document One*
The fables of witchcraft have taken so fast hold and deep root in the heart of man that few can with patience endure the hand and correction of God. For if any adversity, grief, sickness, loss of children, corn or cattle happen to them, they blame witches. As though there were no God that orders all things according to His will; punishing both just and unjust with griefs, plagues and afflictions, as he thinks good; but that certain old women here on earth, called witches, must needs be the cause of all men's calamaties.
*The Discoverie of Witchcraft*, 1584

*Notes*:  'adversity' – misfortune
        'affliction' – distress

1  Whom do people blame when things go wrong?
2  According to Scot, who is really responsible?

Scot also wrote:

*Document Two*
Faithless people are persuaded that neither hail nor snow, thunder nor lightning, rain nor tempestuous winds come from the heavens at the command of God; but are raised by the cunning and power of witches. A clap of thunder or a gale of wind is no sooner heard, but either they run to ring bells, or cry out to burn witches. But certainly it is neither a witch, nor devil, but a glorious God that maketh the thunder. I have read in the scriptures that God maketh the blustering tempests and the whirlwinds. But let me see any of them rebuke and still the sea in time of storm, as Christ did; or raise the stormy wind, as God did with His word, and I will believe in them.
*The Discoverie of Witchcraft*, 1584

*Notes*:  'faithless people' – people who have no faith in God
        'rebuke' – scold

1  Whom do people blame for bad weather?
2  According to Scot, who is really responsible?
3  What does Scot say will make him believe in witches?

According to Scot, God sends people disease and bad weather, and other misfortunes, because they have been wicked. Scot's message is this: when you have a misfortune, don't blame some poor old woman for bewitching you; think, instead, what you have done to deserve God's punishment.

Very few people took any notice of Reginald Scot. Then, nearly twenty years after he had written his book, Queen Elizabeth died and James I became King of England. He believed in witchcraft and he ordered that Scot's book should be burnt. Only a few copies survived. Also, Parliament passed an even more savage law against witchcraft. Later, James changed his mind, and became quite as sceptical as Reginald Scot.

From 1645 to 1646 there was a nasty witch-hunt led by a man called Matthew Hopkins. After that, the persecution of witches died away. The last execution of a witch in Essex was in 1646. The last in England was at Exeter, in 1684. Many people, though, went on believing in witchcraft. Some still do, even today.

# Notes on Money

Today, our coinage is decimalised. All we need to know is:

100 pennies = £1

Before decimalisation, it was like this:

12 pennies = 1 shilling
20 shillings = £1

How many old pennies were there in £1?
How many new pennies equal one shilling?

The abbreviation for shillings was **s**, and for pennies, **d**:

| | |
|---|---|
| Two shillings and eightpence | 2s-8d |
| Fifteen shillings and ninepence | 15s-9d |
| One pound, four shillings and twopence | £1-4s-2d |
| Seven shillings and sixpence | ? |

There was also the halfpenny, or ha'penny (½d), and the farthing (¼d), which was a quarter of a penny. You could have three farthings (¾d):

| | |
|---|---|
| Seventeen shillings and ninepence ha'penny | 17s-9½d |
| Four shillings and threepence farthing | 4s-3¼d |
| Nineteen shillings and elevenpence three farthings | 19s-11¾d |
| Six shillings and tenpence ha'penny | ? |

In Elizabethan times, they often worked in 'marks'. A mark was two thirds of a pound, so it was 13s-4d.

You will quite often come across the amount 6s-8d, because it was half a mark. Another common amount was 3s-4d. What was that?

To change old money into new, it is usually good enough to take the number of shillings and multiply by five. That will give you the answer in new pence. You can usually ignore the old pennies, ha'pennies and farthings. Thus 15s-6d is about 75p.

If you want to be more accurate, count 2.4d as one new penny. Thus 15s-6d is exactly 77½p.

It is much more difficult to decide what Elizabethan money would be worth today. We can, perhaps, learn something from the price of bread. For much of Elizabeth's reign a loaf the size of our large loaf cost one old penny. It was possible, therefore, to buy 240 for £1. In 1985, two such loaves could be bought for £1. This means that when buying bread, the Elizabethan £1 was worth £120, at 1985 prices. When buying sugar, the Elizabethan £1 was worth a lot less. Sugar cost about 1s-0d a pound, or, very roughly, 10p the kilo. In 1985, a kilo of sugar cost 60p. Thus, when buying sugar, the Elizabethan £1 was worth only £6 at 1985 prices. But poor people in Elizabethan times did not use sugar, so its price did not bother them.

Possibly, if you multiply the Elizabethan prices by 100, you will gain a very rough idea of what they would be today.